Foundations 1

Establishing Yourself Upon the Firm Foundation of God's Word

A Basic Study of the Six Foundational Teachings

Found In
Hebrews Chapter Six, Verses One and Two

by
Dr. Carl Forster

Foundations 1

Establishing Your Life Upon The Firm Foundation of God's Word

Printed in the United States of America

ISBN-13:978-1534999541

ISBN-10:153499954X

CONTENTS

INTRODUCTION

The purpose of this course is to establish the Christian believer in the six elementary teachings of Christ as outlined in Hebrews chapter six, verses one and two.

Therefore, leaving the discussion of the elementary principles of Christ, let us go on to perfection, not laying again the foundation of repentance from dead works and of faith toward God, ² of the doctrine of baptisms, of laying on of hands, of resurrection of the dead, and of eternal judgment. **(Hebrews 6:1-2)**

Once we have gained a complete understanding of these six doctrines we will then be able to take each one and apply them to our lives. The results will be life changing. You will then know what it truly means to be an overcomer in Christ Jesus rather than being overcome by the circumstances and situations of life.

WHAT IS A SOLID FOUNDATION?

Why do we as Christians need a foundation? What does it mean to have a solid foundation based on the Word of God in Christ Jesus? To examine these questions, we will turn to the Word of God and to the parable of the wise and foolish builders. *"Therefore everyone who hears these words of Mine and puts them into practice is like a wise man who built his house upon the rock. The rain came down, the streams rose, and the winds blew and beat against the house; yet it did not fall because it had its foundation on the rock. But everyone who hears these words of Mine and does not put them into practice is like a foolish man who built his house upon the sand. The rain came down, the streams rose up, and the winds blew and beat against the house and it fell with a great crash."* (Matthew 7:24-27)

The two houses spoken about in this parable represent people's lives. The storms that came against these houses represent the trials and tribulations that come against all of us in this life. The only difference between these two houses was the foundation hidden beneath the ground just as the foundation or principles that people live by are hidden in the heart of man. What made these people's foundations different? Jesus makes a very clear distinction; the person who takes the words of Jesus and applies them to his life will have a life that can stand anything thrown against it.

Jesus then tells us that the one who hears these words and does not apply them or put them into practice will not be able to withstand when the storms of life come. This parable is primarily making a comparison between believers in Jesus Christ and those who have not yet made Jesus their Lord and Savior. The day we asked Jesus to forgive us our sins and to come into our hearts was the day construction began on a new foundation inside our hearts on which we could now base our new life.

Jesus is called a precious cornerstone. *"Therefore thus saith the Lord God, Behold, I lay in Zion for a foundation a Stone, a tried Stone, a precious cornerstone, a sure foundation; he that believeth shall not make haste."* (Isaiah 28:16) The cornerstone is the first and most important part of a foundation. This stone must be perfect in every way for it is from this stone that the measurements for the entire foundation are taken. If the cornerstone is flawed or imperfect in any way the foundation will be flawed and the entire building will be affected with major structural problems. The same principle is true of our lives.

For our lives to be structurally firm, we need to have Jesus Christ as our cornerstone. Every part of our life needs to come back to Jesus, or in other words, everything we think, say or do needs to be measured or compared to the Word of God. When we do this in our lives we will never be disappointed, dismayed or sorry that we made Jesus our cornerstone. Because Jesus is our Creator God, He will supply whatever we need to fulfill His purpose in our lives. With Jesus as our foundation, we will be able to build our lives to the full potential of what God has for us.

The Apostle Paul, in his letter to the believers in Corinth, states, *"For no other foundation can anyone lay than that which is laid, which is Jesus Christ."* **(1 Corinthians 3:11)** We are clearly told in this scripture that Jesus is to be our *only* foundation. Can people have a foundation other than that of Jesus? The answer is yes; Mohammed, Buddha, and New Age teachings are a few common to our times. Many teachings from these groups seem to be good for they typically try to discipline your mind and your body to certain rules. These rules usually place high value on human life and to living in harmony with one another. This sounds wonderful ... only it doesn't work! Only if there is a change of heart within the inner part of man, can there be a permanent change in the actions of the mind and the body. Religions like the ones listed above aim to conform people to their rules.

The rationale is that if the outside of the person is changed it will then affect the inner man, which is the mind and spirit of that individual. This theory makes as much sense as attempting to set an alcoholic free from alcoholism by solely taking him off the street, giving him a shower and dressing him in a business suit. Has this man really experienced any change in his life other than smelling better? Given enough time this man will return back to his drunken state in the streets. This example depicts the best results religion can attain - temporary alteration.

By definition, religion simply means: attempts through which mankind tries to reach God on his/her own through works. Alternately, true Christianity acknowledges that God has already provided a way to Himself through the death, burial, and resurrection of His own Son, Jesus the Christ. When your life is founded on Jesus it is not based on religion but on relationship. Since our relationship to God is based on the finished work of Jesus, it is not by our own works that we are saved, but rather by faith or trust in what Jesus has already done for us.

When we receive Jesus as our Lord and Savior, a wonderful thing happens on the inside of us. *"I will give you a new heart and put a new spirit within you; I will take the heart of stone out of your flesh and give you a heart of flesh. I will put My Spirit within you and cause you to walk in My statutes, and you will keep My judgments and do them."* **(Ezekiel 36:26-27)** We are given a new heart and a new spirit. We are completely changed on the inside. Instead of having a cold, unloving, uncompassionate heart we now have a warm, loving and compassionate heart which embodies a desire to see others have the same joy and peace that we now have in Jesus.

This scripture also tells us that God's Spirit also comes and makes His home in us to counsel and direct us in our daily walk. Over a period of time this inner change will begin to affect both the mind and the body because we are spirit beings that possess a mind and live in a body. This is how a relationship with Jesus causes permanent change in a person's life. God goes to the root of the problem and begins His work there, in the inner part of man - his heart.

We can now clearly see that our lives must be built on Jesus Christ. He is a firm foundation, a tried or tested foundation that will never fail us. As we base our entire life on the truths of God's Word, we will have a foundation that will stand up to the most furious storms of life. With Jesus as our cornerstone, we can be excited and prepared for everything that will happen to us in this life and in eternity.

CHAPTER 1: REPENTANCE FROM ACTS THAT LEAD TO DEATH

"Therefore, leaving the discussion of the elementary principles of Christ, let us go on to perfection, not laying again the foundation of <u>repentance from dead works</u> and of faith toward God, ² of the doctrine of baptisms, of laying on of hands, of resurrection of the dead, and of eternal judgment." **(Hebrews 6:1-2)**

In the New Testament the word **repent** comes from the Greek word, **"metanoein,"** which means to change one's mind (this is an internal change). In the Old Testament the word, **"repent",** means to turn back, to return, or to so turn (this is in reference to an external action). If we combine the Old and New Testament definitions of the word repent, we find that God has given us a complete picture of this word; which means that true repentance, when it begins in the heart (internal), will eventually become evident in our lives to those around us (external). Repentance is not a feeling or an emotion, but a decision that is made within our heart and then works out to every part of our lives.

In **Luke 15:11-32** we find the parable of the prodigal son. The younger son, not being content with his situation of life, asks his father for his share of the inheritance. His father, being a loving father, grants his son's request and divides up the inheritance. One thing many Christians do not understand is that God will allow us to do what we want and He will not stop us if we choose to go in the wrong direction.

In this parable, we see that the younger son squandered all his inheritance on wild living until it was completely used up. How many people today are squandering the gifts and talents that God has given them in the world, rather than using them for what they were designed for - the advancement of the kingdom of God and to honor and glorify God.

Next, the son tried to remedy his situation by becoming a servant to a citizen of that particular country, however his needs were still not met. This son's example depicts a person in total bondage (slavery to the world) without fulfillment or happiness in life. It was at this point that the son came to a realization of the futility of his way of thinking. The son recognized that he had made a terrible mistake, and decided (made a conscious decision) to return to his father and confess his mistake (sin).

Many times we have to hit rock bottom before we will look up and confess our wrongdoing to our Heavenly Father in order that we might be forgiven and restored back into fellowship with Him. Do you know what the father's attitude was as he saw his son returning from afar off? The Bible says in verse twenty that the father was filled with compassion, and that he ran to his son, threw his arms around him and kissed him. Nowhere in this account do you hear the father telling the son, "You had better not do this again," or, "I will give you one more chance and that's all!" What we do see is full acceptance of the son by the father. Jesus gave us this parable so that we might understand the heart of our Heavenly Father, who wants to forgive us and bring us back into fellowship with Him.

When we turn to God in repentance He will forgive us. *"If we confess our sins, God is faithful and just to forgive us our sins and to cleanse us from all unrighteousness."* **(1 John 1:9)** The word *forgive* in this scripture literally means that it is forgotten. When God forgives us He no longer remembers that we did anything wrong, and hence can never hold it against us at a future time. The confession of sin is the main part of true repentance.

To repent or to have a change of mind accompanied by some corresponding action, one must realize that he or she is doing something wrong and correction is needed. This is the first step of an unbeliever when coming to the point of salvation - the realization that he is a sinner and the need to repent. The word *salvation* actually means to be saved or to be rescued. What have we been rescued from? We have been rescued from the penalty of sin as we are told in **Romans 6:23,** *"That the wages of sin is death."* This death that is spoken of does not refer to just physical death but also to spiritual death, meaning eternal separation from God. Since everyone who has ever lived has sinned, we all need to repent of our sins and turn back to God.

What brings a lost sinner to a point of repentance?
"It is the kindness (goodness) of God that leads us to repentance." (Romans 2:4) What is the goodness of God? It is all wrapped up in God's Son, Jesus Christ, who is God's gift to mankind. God will only lead us, He will never drive us or force us to follow Him. He would rather we draw to Him because of His goodness and kindness because He truly loves us. We are often instructed to proclaim the Gospel of Jesus Christ to the world. The word *gospel* means, "good news."

The good news lies in the fact that God sent His only Son to the earth, who although He lived a sinless life, was rejected and abused, crucified with criminals, died and was placed in a tomb. Three days later He rose from the dead, victorious over sin and death, having paid the price for our sins.

Initially this may not sound like good news, but once you realize that we each individually deserved this punishment, it becomes very good news, because Jesus bore it for us personally. This is the message that we are to proclaim to the lost. Most of the lost know they are not in a right relationship with God, but what they do not know is how to be rescued or saved from their sins. Praise God we have the answer **- FAITH IN JESUS CHRIST!**

First comes repentance, then faith in God, but is there more than one type of repentance? The following verse shows us that there is only one kind of repentance that leads to salvation. ***"For Godly sorrow produces repentance to salvation, not to be regretted; but the sorrow of the world produces death."*** **(2 Corinthians 7:10)**

The above scripture identifies that it takes a special kind of sorrow to lead us unto repentance which results in salvation. This sorrow comes from God. Before true repentance can take place, the Holy Spirit begins to convict the unbeliever of sin. During this time, a great sadness or distress comes upon them. They will experience a sense of being lost, an emptiness, and a feeling of guilt and shame in the sight of God, as well as a realization that if they continue in the same direction as before, all they have to look forward to is eternal separation from God.

This conviction grows in intensity until the unbeliever comes to a point of decision regarding this question, "Am I going to continue to live separated from God so I may enjoy the pleasures of this world for a season, and when this life ends depart to the fires of hell? OR, am I going to repent, submit my will to God's will, receive Jesus into my heart and become a member of God's family, and when this life ends continue in the joy and peace that comes with being a child of God in eternity?"

If at this point the unbeliever chooses to remain in sin, the conviction of the Holy Spirit will begin to lessen. God does not force anyone to become born again. God only provides the opportunity or way of escape from the kingdom of darkness to the kingdom of Jesus Christ. Now if the person chooses to receive Jesus, the Holy Spirit then comes into that person's life, empowering him to be able to repent and change the direction of his live.

This process of repenting from sins and accepting Jesus to save them is referred to as the, "New Birth" or being "Born Again." It is at this point that God takes out their heart of stone that is cold, unloving and unable to repent and replaces it with a heart of flesh which is warm, loving, and merciful, and receptive to the leading of the Holy Spirit.

The last part of **2 Corinthians 7:10** tells of worldly sorrow leading to death. To illustrate the difference between Godly sorrow and worldly sorrow, I will use an excellent example involving my younger brother, Robert, and a previous employment he held. Robert worked for a large gasoline distributor in the accounting department. It was his job to monitor how much fuel each gas station received and the payment schedules.

During a routine check Robert found that one station was short several thousand dollars on a payment. Upon a careful back check, Robert found that this particular station manager had actually short-paid the company approximately $50,000 over a period of six months.

Immediately the police were called in to arrest the station manager, and Robert was a witness to the arrest. Upon arriving, they found the man crying. As the handcuffs were being put on the man, an officer said an interesting thing to the man, "You're not crying because you're sorry for what you've done, you're only sorry that you were caught." This man, given the same opportunity without being caught, would commit the same crime again. Likewise, the same is true when comparing Godly sorrow and worldly sorrow. When Godly sorrow grips someone it is a sorrow of the heart, and it is only from the heart where true change or repentance can begin to happen.

It is obvious why worldly sorrow will lead to spiritual death - because there has been no real change of heart. Judas the betrayer of Jesus is an excellent example. Judas had Jesus as his own private tutor; walked with him for over three years; witnessed all the miracles that Jesus had performed, and was even one of the disciples empowered and sent out to perform miracles himself.

Yet the true heart of Judas is displayed to us in **John 12:6** which tells us that Judas did not care for the poor, and actually stole money from Jesus for himself. What happened to Judas? Later, after Judas had betrayed Jesus, he felt remorse (worldly sorrow) and hung himself. Jesus, speaking in regard to Judas, told the rest of the disciples, "It would have been better if Judas had never been born." This was in reference to the eternal punishment that Judas would suffer. True repentance of the heart brings a change of mind which then affects our actions.

11

What are dead works?

The word, **"Work,"** gives us the idea of an action, while the word, **"Dead,"** gives us the idea of no life or movement. These words almost seem contrary to each other. When we use these words in the context of scripture we find that, **"Dead works"** is any action performed apart from the guidance or direction of God.

To better understand **"Dead Works,"** let's take a moment and compare them to **"Good Works."** *"For by grace we have been saved through faith and that not in yourselves; it is the gift of God not of works, lest anyone would boast. For we are His workmanship, created in Christ Jesus for <u>good works</u>, which God prepared beforehand that we should walk in them."* **(Ephesians 2:8-10)** We need to realize that good works cannot save us; for if they could save us there would be no need for faith in Jesus our Savior.

Many people in the world try to please God through works such as:

1.) Giving money to charitable organizations
2.) Helping the needy or sick and poor
3.) Trying to live a good moral life
4.) Going to church

In this scripture, God tells us in no uncertain terms who the Boss is, and what works we are to do. God created us; we are His workmanship, His handiwork. Who are we to present our own feeble efforts to God expecting to please Him? The Bible says in **Isaiah 64:6**, *"Our own righteousness are as filthy rags in God's sight."* So what works are pleasing to God? Verse 10 of Ephesians 2 gives us the answer.

In Christ, we are to perform good works that God has prepared for us. These works are not ours, but rather they are God's purpose and plan working through us. Therefore, we cannot boast in them, because as servants of God we are performing the duties that our Master has set out before us.

Notice that these good works have been prepared in advance. God knows exactly what He is doing. He knows our gifts, our limitations, and our abilities. When God gives us a job to do, we can be sure that we can bring it to fruition through the power and instruction of the Holy Spirit who lives in us.

To sum up the doctrine of Repentance from Dead Works, we understand that it means a turning or change of mind from actions performed apart from God. Once this is accomplished, we can then focus our attention on performing the plan (Good Works) that God has prepared for our lives. We then can begin to enjoy the fruit of it as well as experience the peace and joy of doing our Master's will here on this earth. Now that we have truly repented from our sins and are no longer separated from God, we can turn our attention to the second elementary doctrine: **FAITH TOWARDS GOD**.

STUDY QUESTIONS (INTRODUCTION - WHAT IS OUR FOUNDATION)

1. In the parable of the wise and foolish builders, what was different between the two houses?_____

_____

2. What do the houses represent?_____

_____

3. Who should our foundation be and why?_____

_____

_____

_____

(LESSON 1 - REPENTANCE FROM ACTS THAT LEAD TO DEATH)

1. What does the word repent mean?_____

_____

2. According to **Romans 2:4**, the _____ of God leads us to repentance.

3. Is repentance a feeling, emotion, or a decision? Explain your answer._____

_____

4. What are dead works?_____

_____

_____

5. Can you list some dead works that you did before receiving Jesus?_____

_____

_____

6. Why do you think it is important for a Christian to repent from dead works?_____

_____

_____

_____

Read Hebrews 11:1 to prepare for next week's discussion entitled *"Faith Toward God."*

NOTES

CHAPTER 2: FAITH TOWARD GOD

"Therefore, leaving the discussion of the elementary principles of Christ, let us go on to perfection, not laying again the foundation of repentance from dead works and of <u>faith toward God,</u> [2] of the doctrine of baptisms, of laying on of hands, of resurrection of the dead, and of eternal judgment." **(Hebrews 6:1-2)**

This is the second foundational doctrine which we will study. Please note the progression from lesson one; the fact that unless we have experienced true repentance, we cannot have faith towards God. Why is this true? In chapter one, we learned that repentance means a change of mind, as well as a physical change of the direction of our lives.

The following scripture came at the beginning of Jesus' ministry. ***"From that time Jesus began to preach and say 'Repent for the kingdom of heaven is at hand.'"*** **(Matthew 4:17)** Jesus said this because people have to have a change of heart. They must take their eyes off themselves and their religious rituals and fix them on Jesus, so that they might then by faith become part of the kingdom of God. We still must do this today! Are you ready to begin to grow in faith towards God?

What is faith?

The word *faith* in the New Testament, comes from the Greek word **"*pistis*,"** which means persuasion or moral conviction, and is translated: faith, assurance, belief, believe. An excellent Biblical definition is found in the book of Hebrews. ***"Now faith is the substance of things hoped for, the evidence of things not seen."*** **(Hebrews 11:1)**

We see that faith originates from the unseen realm or the spirit realm. To take this a step further, faith originates in the spirit realm and is then manifested in the natural or physical realm. The evidence of true faith at work in our lives, is proved by when we see things happen in the natural. For example, God spoke and the world was created over a period of seven days. God spoke in the spirit realm, and that which was unseen became substance.

In the opening pages of Genesis, we see God speaking our world and everything we can see into existence. Before that there was nothing and out of the nothing, God brought forth something. That "something" is what we can see today, as evidence of God's faith. Faith is real. It effects people, events and even our future.

Even though we as believers see God's creative power at work in the world, the people of the world cannot see the creator God. Why? It is because unbelievers cannot understand faith. The unbelievers in the world say, "Show me and I will believe," but God says, "Believe and I will reveal or show myself to you."

Hebrews 11:6 tells us, *"Without faith it is impossible to please God because anyone who comes to Him must believe (have faith) that He exists and that He rewards those who earnestly seeks Him."* This entire scripture is based on faith, specifically faith in the fact that God exists. Really, this makes a lot of sense. Would you approach a God that you don't believe exists? It would be like going to the door of a house to visit a person you know does not live there. This is why a relationship with God must begin by faith. Faith is believing that God exists and that He rewards those who seek after Him. What is the reward? - eternal life with our creator God.

In **Luke 18:1-8**, we find the parable of the persistent widow and the unjust judge. We can see this as a picture of the world system. The unjust judge represents the unsaved people, the rulers of this world. The widow represents the Christians, those who have turned their lives over to Jesus. The parable is simple enough. The widow comes to the unjust judge with one plea, "Grant me justice from my adversary." The judge refuses to help her. However, because of her persistence, he grants her request stating, "He cares not about men nor fears God." Verse 1 of chapter 18 tells us the reason why Jesus told this parable; so we would always pray and not give up. This widow, even though the circumstances indicated that her request would not be granted, remained steadfast.

Every time she was denied her request, she would go home and fall before God in prayer and supplication, knowing that her God was in ultimate control of the situation. As we see in the parable, her persistence paid off. She was granted her request. Often we as Christians appear to be the underdog in the natural, but in the spirit realm we are overcomers. At the end of the parable Jesus makes a powerful statement in verse 8b; *"However when the Son of man comes will He find faith on the earth?"* The widow's prayers were based on faith, or the assurance and certainty that God was on her side and that He would grant her request because she was praying according to His will.

In the physical realm this widow never had a chance, but in the spirit realm she was victorious by faith. Because she stood on this victory, it then manifested in the natural realm. Going against all odds, the unjust judge changed his mind granting the widow's request.

Faith comes into action when all the natural circumstances say it is impossible! *"We walk by faith, not by sight."* **(2 Corinthians 5:7)** As we have already read, we as believers cannot live or be controlled by what we see, or the circumstances that we find ourselves in. We must come to the complete realization that the circumstances and situations in which we find ourselves originate in an unseen spirit realm.

In other words, to deal with these circumstances means to cause changes in the spirit realm, so that the natural realm, or that which we see, will be affected. We find in the case of the persistent widow that it was persistent prayer combined with faith that moved the hand of God. To live by faith is to know that God is on our side, and as we submit to His will, God will work His perfect plan out in our lives.

Romans 10:17 tells us, *"So then faith comes by hearing, and hearing by the word of God."* By this scripture it would first appear that for us to grow in faith all we need to do is to listen to the Word of God, but in reality, listening is not enough. If you remember from **Matthew 7:24-26** the story of the two houses, which represented two different individuals, each one heard the word but only the one who acted upon it stood strong when the storms came. The word "hearing" in the above scripture means much more than listening. It means to perceive or understand what is being said leading to an action based upon what has been heard. So, real faith can only come into action when we have heard the will of God for a given situation.

There are Two Kinds or Types of Faith

The first type of faith we are going to study is "Seed Faith." In the following scripture, we have a clear statement showing us that God gives each believer a measure or a portion of faith. *"God has dealt to each one a measure of faith."* **(Romans 12:3b)** Why does God do this? First, we must realize that God is a "no-nonsense" God. He gives us what we need to accomplish His will. The context of the above scripture points to each believer having a purpose in the body of Christ.

God gives each of us the faith necessary to function in the gifts He has given us. (We discuss in depth the Gifts in Foundations 2.) In **Matthew 17:20** Jesus tells us, *"If you have faith as small as a mustard seed and you say to this mountain, 'move from here to there,' and it will move. Nothing will be impossible for you."* Now the mustard seed is one of the smallest seeds known, yet when planted can grow to the size of a tree. The point Jesus is making is the fact that we all have faith as believers.

God has given faith to us at the new birth. Faith is trusting God at His Word; the Word that He has revealed to us.

Seed faith is a type of faith that we can grow in our lives. *"For in the Gospel the righteousness of God has been revealed from faith to faith, just as it has been written, "The just shall live by faith."* **(Romans 1:17)** We see here God telling us that we can grow from faith to faith. How is this accomplished? We have already stated that faith is trusting God at His Word. When we as believers pray and read God's Word, we are open to have a spiritual truth revealed to us. When we then apply this truth to our lives by faith and see it work, we come to a new level of faith.

As God reveals further truths or principles and by faith we apply these things and see God bringing them to fruition, we are growing from faith to faith. It is only as the Word of God is revealed to our hearts, that we by faith can apply it to our lives, and therefore keep growing in faith.

To summarize: To grow in Seed Faith we must complete three distinct steps:
1.) We hear a truth from God's Word
2.) We receive that Word or acknowledge that it is true
3.) We apply it to our lives

It is easy to understand now how we can grow in levels of faith, but remember this faith is like climbing a ladder. You take it one step at a time, one truth at a time, climbing higher, understanding more fully the truths of God's Word.

The second type of faith that we will discuss is the gift of faith.

Observe the following scripture specially looking for the gift of faith. *"But the manifestation of the Spirit is given to each one for the profit of all: for to one is given the word of wisdom through the Spirit, to another the word of knowledge through the same Spirit, to another FAITH by the same Spirit, to another gifts of healings by the same Spirit, to another the working of miracles, to another prophecy, to another discerning of spirits, to another different kinds of tongues, to another the interpretation of tongues. But one and the same Spirit works all these things, distributing to each one individually as He wills."* **(1 Corinthians 12:7-11)**

We see according to the scripture that it is God who distributes the gift of faith, according to His will. We do not have direct control over this type of faith. We need the gift of faith when our own faith comes to an end. There is a limit to the faith by which we live, but there is no limit to God's faith. To understand more fully the difference between the measure of faith given to each believer and the gift of faith, we can use nature as an example.

If we compared our Christian lives to a tree, we can see that as each year passes, the tree grows. We as believers, as we go through seasons in our lives, will grow from faith to faith. That measure of faith God has given to us grows in us as we believe God from situation to situation. But just like the tree, our faith has a limit at any given time. Yes, it is continually growing, but there is a limit of our own faith to believe God in a particular situation.

If we measure the height of a tree at a given time, then measure it a year later, we can see the difference in height. Can a tree grow six feet in one day? This may seem like a silly question, and we already know the answer. The measure of faith is much like a tree in that it grows steadily from season to season, and in our lives from faith to faith.

Now what happens when we come to a situation or circumstance that we do not have the faith to overcome? In other words, what happens when we come to the end of our ability to believe? This is where the gift of faith comes into operation. God reaches down and supernaturally empowers us with the gift of faith to accomplish His will. An excellent example from the word to demonstrate the gift of faith is the account of Moses parting the Red Sea **(Exodus 14:15-31)**. When Moses and the Israelites came to the Red Sea, the natural situation said that they were trapped.

Moses knew by the gift of faith that he had that God would provide a way. ***"And Moses said unto the people, "Fear ye not, stand still, and see the salvation of the Lord, which He will show to you today: For the Egyptians whom ye have seen today, ye shall see them again no more forever."*** **(Exodus 14:13)** As we read this account, we see God telling Moses to stretch out his staff over the sea. By faith Moses obeys. Supernaturally God reaches down from heaven and parts the sea, allowing the Israelites to cross and the Egyptians to drown. We see in this account the faith of Moses coming to an end, and the imparting of the gift of faith to accomplish God's purpose.

Daniel in the lion's den **(Daniel 6:1-28)**, and Peter walking on water **(Matthew 14:22-31),** are two more examples of the gift of faith operating in a believer's life.

CONCLUSION TO FAITH TOWARD GOD

Faith is truly trusting God at His word for His provision and protection; knowing that He is greater than any problem or situation that we can possibly have in this life. **Romans 1:17** talks of growing from faith to faith. As we trust God in a situation of life and overcome, this becomes a springboard to believe God for an even bigger situation; we grow from faith to faith. If we are in the will of God and our own faith comes to its limit, then God will provide us with the gift of faith to get the job done to His honor and glory. **(See Hebrews 12:2 and Philippians 1:6)**

STUDY QUESTIONS (LESSON 2 - FAITH TOWARD GOD)

1. The Greek word *pistis* can be translated _____, _____, _____, or_____.

2. In the parable of the persistent widow, why did she need faith?_____
_____
_____
_____

3. According to **2 Corinthians 5:7**, we walk by _____and not by _____.

4. Read **John 20:24-29**. Why can we say that Thomas lacked faith at that particular point of his life?
_____
_____
_____

5. According to **Romans 10:17**, how does faith come?_____
_____

And by whom does it come?_____
_____

6. What are three steps to grow by faith?

1)_____

2)_____

3)_____

7. What is the difference between faith we live by and the gift of faith?_____
_____
_____

8. If someone asked you to explain in a few words what faith toward God is, what would you say? _____
_____
_____

NOTES

CHAPTER 3: DOCTRINE OF BAPTISMS

"Therefore leaving the discussion of the elementary principles of Christ, let us go onto perfection; not laying again the foundation of repentance from dead works, and of faith toward God, of <u>the doctrine of baptisms</u>, and of laying on of hands, and of resurrection of the dead, and of eternal judgment." **(Hebrews 6:1-2)**

As we continue our study of the six elementary teachings of Christ, we see in verse 2 of Hebrews 6 the word "baptisms." Notice the word is plural, obviously pointing to the fact that more than one type of baptism is presented in the Word of God.

In our study we are going to look at four different baptisms:
1.) Baptism of John the Baptist
2.) Christian baptism
3.) Baptism of the Holy Spirit
4.) Baptism of suffering

Before we begin our study of baptisms, a clear definition of the word must be made. The Greek word for **baptism** is **"baptize"** and means to fully wet, to cover wholly with a fluid, or to dip. Already questions may be entering your mind concerning water baptism and practices in some churches. These will be addressed later in our study.

Baptism of John the Baptist

John the Baptist was the last of the true Old Testament prophets. John was born about six months before Jesus and began his ministry before Jesus. *"As it is written in the prophets, 'Behold, I send My messenger before thy face, which shall prepare thy way before thee, the voice of one crying in the wilderness, Prepare ye the way of the Lord, make his paths straight.'*

John did baptize in the wilderness, and preach the baptism of repentance for the remission of sins. And there went out unto him all the land of Judea, and they of Jerusalem, and were all baptized of him in the river Jordan, confessing their sins.

And John was clothed with camel's hair, and with a girdle of a skin about his loins; and he did eat locusts and wild honey; And preached, saying, 'There cometh one mightier than I after me, the latchet of whose shoes I am not worthy to stoop down and unloosen. I indeed have baptized you with water: but He shall baptize you with the Holy Ghost.'" **(Mark 1:2-8)**

Mark gives us an excellent picture of who John the Baptist was and the purpose for his coming. First of all, John was sent to proclaim the coming of the Messiah (twice in the above passage it speaks of preparing the way). How did God accomplish this through John? For centuries the Jews had offered up animal sacrifices for the covering of their sins. It came to a point where the religious leaders taught the people that as long as they were descendants of Abraham and offered up sacrifices, they were able to enter the kingdom of heaven.

The people thought that they could be saved by their ancestry and religious rituals. **Romans 3:20** tells us, *"No one becomes righteous in God's sight by obeying (following the letter of the law) but rather through the law one becomes conscious of sin."* The law was really put into place to point people to the need of a Messiah, (Savior) Jesus.

We see here that John preached a baptism of repentance. *"He (John) went into all the country around the Jordan, preaching a baptism of repentance for the forgiveness of sins."* **(Luke 3:3)** We learned earlier in our study that true repentance means a change of direction in a person's life. As John preached, people came to a point of realization that even though they tried to keep the ordinances of the law that they still were not worthy in God's sight. They came to John and were baptized confessing their sins.

The reason John baptized them was that as they would go under the water they would be leaving their old ways of life. As they came out of the water, it became a point in time when they were to go in a different direction in their lives. Was there any real power in John's baptism that would cause permanent change in a person's life?

"I baptize you with water for repentance. But after me will come one (Jesus) who is more powerful than I whose sandals I am not fit to carry. He (Jesus) will baptize you with the Holy Spirit and with fire." **(Matthew 3:11)** John compares himself to Jesus, pointing out that while his baptism is only of water, the baptism Jesus offers is that of the Holy Spirit and fire. If John's baptism was only temporary with no lasting impact, then why did God have him do it?

What God did through John's baptism of repentance was to prepare the hearts of the people. It was through John's baptism that the people were made ready for the coming Messiah. As stated earlier in our study, before we can have faith towards God, we must have a repentant heart; a heart that will be open to the life changing work of the Holy Spirit.

The evidence of the purpose of the ministry of John the Baptist is found in Matthew as Jesus spoke to the unbelieving religious leaders. ***"For John (the Baptist) came to show you the way of righteousness and you did not believe him, but the tax collectors and the prostitutes did. And even after you (the religious leaders) saw this, you did not repent and believe him (John the Baptist)."*** **(Matthew 21:32)** Jesus speaks of John showing the way of righteousness.

Why could the religious leaders not believe? They were not willing to repent, and because of this they could not believe in the Messiah, Jesus Christ. Their hearts were hard and therefore could not receive the promise of salvation through faith in Jesus Christ.

Can the baptism of John save you?

The answer is no. John's baptism was a baptism of repentance. John came proclaiming the soon-coming Savior, to prepare the hearts of the people to receive Christ as their personal Lord and Savior. However, the principle of John's baptism is still used today. As we are leading an unsaved person in the salvation prayer, the first thing we do is have that person confess they are a sinner and the need to repent.

This decision prepares the heart of that person to release faith towards God, and allows Jesus to come and live in their hearts. Just as John's baptism of repentance prepared the Jewish nation for the coming of Jesus, repentance prepares the heart of the unsaved person to receive Jesus. Once Jesus makes His home in us, we can be sure there will be a permanent change in our lives, both now and in eternity.

Christian Baptism

There are six major reasons according to the Word of God that point out the necessity for a Christian to be baptized:

    1.) To fulfill all righteousness

    2.) As an act of obedience

    3.) To identify us with Christ

4.) As a public confession

5.) To have a good conscience toward God

6.) For spiritual circumcision of the heart

To Fulfill All Righteousness

Observe the following scripture to see the interaction between John the Baptist and Jesus. *"Then Jesus came from Galilee to John at the Jordan to be baptized by him. And John tried to prevent Him, saying, "I have need to be baptized by You, and are You coming to me?" But Jesus answered and said to him, "Permit it to be so now, for us to fulfill all righteousness." Then Jesus, when He had been baptized, came up immediately from the water; and behold, the heavens were opened to Him, and the Spirit of God descending like a dove and alighted upon Him. And suddenly a voice came from heaven, saying, "This is My beloved Son in Whom I am well pleased."* (Matthew 3:13-17)

It is evident that John recognized who Jesus was-that is, the Son of God. We see this in the fact that John wanted Jesus to baptize him. Yet Jesus makes an unusual statement in verse 15, stating that it will fulfill all righteousness. This statement is alluding to the fact that Jesus was the fulfillment, or the completion, of the Old Covenant which is found in the Old Testament of the Bible.

There are over 700 prophecies or predictions concerning the coming, the life, the ministry, the death and the resurrection of Jesus. Verse 17 tells us that a voice proclaimed from heaven, *"This is My Son, in whom I am well pleased."* God the Father spoke this because it was both a fulfillment of Old Testament scripture, as well as an act of obedience.

As an Act of Obedience

Jesus was perfect in every way, so why then did He allow Himself to be baptized? *"For to this you were called, because Christ also suffered for us, leaving us an example, that you should follow His steps: Who committed no sin, nor was guile found in His mouth."* (1 Peter 2:21-22)

The baptism of John was a baptism of repentance. Did Jesus need to repent of sins? The answer is no. Jesus was perfect in every way. The angels at His birth proclaimed to the shepherds that Jesus would be called, *"Emmanuel which means God with us."* (Matthew 1:23) Jesus was an example to us that we are to follow His steps.

When Jesus was baptized He was establishing a pattern of behavior for Christians. We see that Christian baptism in part is an outward act of obedience.

To Identify Us with Christ

The word **Christian** literally means "Christ-like one." So again we see the need to follow the example that Christ has given us, but not just as an outward act of obedience. *"Or do you not know that as many of us as were baptized into Christ Jesus were baptized into His death? Therefore we were buried with Him through baptism into death that just as Christ was raised from the dead by the glory of the Father, even so we also should walk in newness of life."* **(Romans 6:3-4)**

As we go down into the baptismal waters we are identifying ourselves with the death, and burial, of Jesus. As we come up and out of the water, we are identifying ourselves with the resurrected Christ.

How does identifying (or understanding) the death, burial, and resurrection of Christ give us newness of life? The answer lies in the physical condition of Jesus. When Jesus died His body bore the marks of a man who was a criminal. Crucifixion was reserved for only the worst of the worst criminals. Jesus was the Son of God, and yet suffered and died as a criminal. He did this for the entire world. For in suffering and dying the way He did, Jesus took the punishment for all of our sins. As we go under the baptismal waters, we are realizing that Jesus suffered and bore the punishment for our sins. **Romans 4:25** tells us, *"Jesus was turned over to death for our sins and raised to life for our justification."*

While under the water, we see those sins that Jesus suffered for us being left behind in the baptismal waters. As we come out of the water, just as Jesus rose from the dead, we too can walk in a newness and freedom knowing that our old sins and habits no longer have any hold over us. Jesus has set us free from the bondage of sin and death just as He himself had the victory over sin and death for us. As we Identify ourselves with Christ through water baptism, a realization of the power of God rises up within us to overcome areas of sin in our lives.

As a Public Confession

Christian baptism is a public demonstration of the fact that you are committing your life to be a disciple of Jesus. For us in North American culture, this may not appear to be that significant. If a Jew receives Jesus into his heart and is baptized, often the family will have a funeral for that person and cuts off all relations. In the Moslem culture a person who receives Christ and is baptized often faces heavy persecution, and may even face death for his or her faith.

In these two cultures it is a major decision to be baptized publicly. Thank God that these people can say as the Apostle Paul says in **Philippians 1:21**, *"To live is Christ, to die is gain."* The promise of eternal life far outweighs physical death.

To Have a Good Conscience Towards God

One thing that we need to realize is that water baptism has nothing to do with the cleansing of our physical body, but rather a working within the soul (mind) of man. *"And this water symbolizes baptism that now saves you also - not the removal of dirt from the outside but the pledge of a good conscience toward God."* **(1 Peter 3:21)**

Jesus made this very clear when He spoke of the religious leaders of His time and called them whitewashed tombs. Jesus pointed out to them that they washed before eating and wore all the right clothes so that on the surface they looked like Godly people, but on the inside they were full of hypocrisy, envy, strife, and jealousy. Even though they looked very much alive in a relationship with God, they were like the dead people's bones within the whitewashed tombs.

Whenever Jesus spoke He always went to the root of the problem: *"For out of the abundance of the heart the mouth speaks."* **(Matthew 12:34b)** . It was not that the actions of the religious leaders were wrong within themselves, but rather the attitudes and intents of the heart behind the actions. In other words, it is from our conscience that actions originate. Water baptism is a time in which we can have an answer of a good conscience before God. How is this possible?

We first must acknowledge that before we received Jesus, we never did anything with a pure conscience. There was always a hidden agenda, a selfish ambition, a false motive involved in every action we performed

Then we received Jesus who gave us a new heart which cleansed us of our sin nature, which in turn gave us new motives- motives that were no longer self-centered, but Christ centered. Just as Jesus gave himself completely for us, we in turn are to give ourselves completely to others. No hidden agendas or selfish ambitions, but with a pure conscience, knowing that God is watching out for us.

When we are water baptized we are acknowledging what Jesus has done in our lives; the new nature of God that lives within us has given us a good conscience. When Satan accuses us of having wrong intents, we can clearly tell him Jesus paid the price for us to have a good conscience, and we acknowledged this fact when we were baptized.

For Spiritual Circumcision of the Heart

We have a new nature once we receive Christ. *"Therefore, if anyone is in Christ, he is a new creation; old things have passed away; behold, all things have become new."* **(2 Corinthians 5:17)**

It is an internal change within us. How can this internal change happen within us? How can this internal change work out in a practical way to the outside of our lives? The miracle of the new nature happened instantly when we asked Jesus to come and live inside of us.

But what about our old nature that used to be within us? Scripture tells us that it is now gone if we are in Christ. But often we find ourselves doing many of the same "old nature things" that are now supposed to be gone because of the new nature within us. This is because these are "old nature" habits. Many times we don't even realize we are doing them, but Jesus has a solution to deal with these "old nature" habits.

First, we need to recognize that these habits are enemies to our new nature and that they need to be destroyed (replaced by Godly habits). *"Then Moses stretched out his hand over the sea; and the LORD caused the sea to go back by a strong east wind all that night, and made the sea into dry land, and the waters were divided. So the children of Israel went into the midst of the sea on the dry ground, and the waters were a wall to them on their right hand and on their left. And the Egyptians pursued and went after them into the midst of the sea, all Pharaoh's horses, his men, his chariots, and his horsemen.*

Now it came to pass, in the morning watch, that the LORD looked down upon the army of the Egyptians through the pillar of fire and cloud, and He troubled the army of Egyptians. And He took off their chariot wheels, so that they drove them with difficulty; and the Egyptians said, "Let us flee from the face of Israel, for the LORD fights for them against the Egyptians." Then the LORD said to Moses, "Stretch out your hand over the sea that the waters may come back upon the Egyptians, on their chariots, and on their horsemen." And Moses stretched out his hand over the sea; and when the morning appeared, the water returned to its full depth, while the Egyptians were fleeing into it. So the LORD overthrew the Egyptians in the midst of the sea. Then the waters returned and covered the chariots, the horsemen, and all the army of Pharaoh that came into the sea after them. Not so much as one of them remained. But the children of Israel had walked on dry land in the midst of the sea, and the waters were a wall to them on their right hand and on their left. So the LORD saved Israel that day out of the hand of the Egyptians, and Israel saw the Egyptians dead on the seashore. Thus Israel saw the great work which the LORD had done in Egypt; so the people feared the LORD, and believed the LORD and His servant Moses." **(Exodus 14:21-31)**

As we read this portion of scripture we need to see it as a type of or picture of water baptism. We see Moses leading the people of Israel between the waters of the Red Sea. The Egyptians follow in pursuit of the Israelites to destroy them. What happens to the Egyptians? They are utterly destroyed by the water, never again to be able to physically assault the Israelites.

To understand this in the context of Christian baptism we need to see the Israelites as a Christian and the Red Sea as the waters of baptism. What followed the Israelites into the Red Sea? The Egyptians, who represent our "old nature" habits we had in the world. Who came out of the water? The Israelites. And who remained drowned in the water? The Egyptians. As we enter the waters of baptism our old " sin nature " habits follow us in.

By faith in the permanent life changing work of Jesus, those old habits are destroyed within the waters of baptism. Our hearts are spiritually circumcised. In other words, our "old nature" habits are peeled back or revealed as what they truly are - enemies to us and to the new nature that lives within us. Once they are recognized for what they are they can be easily defeated in the name of Jesus, who is above every ruler and authority both here on earth, and in heaven above us.

Just as physical circumcision was a sign that you were a follower of the one true God in the Old Testament under the Old Covenant, baptism is a sign that you are a follower of the one true God under the New Covenant.

WHAT ARE THE CONDITIONS FOR CHRISTIAN BAPTISM?

A) Repenting

"Now when they heard this, they were pricked in their heart, and said unto Peter and to the rest of the apostles, men and brethren what shall we do? Then Peter said unto them, Repent, and be baptized every one of you in the name of Jesus Christ for the remission of sins, and ye shall receive the gift of the Holy Ghost." **(Acts 2:37-38)**

After the gospel had been preached the people were convicted of their sins and cried out to Peter, **"What must we do to be saved?"** What was Peter's response? "Repent and be baptized in the name of Jesus and you shall be forgiven your sins." The Greek word for **repent** means, "to have a change of mind." So what Peter was really saying was, "turn from your life of sin and be baptized to prove outwardly you want that change of mind."

B) Believing

"And he said unto them, Go ye into all the world, and preach the gospel to every creature. He that believeth and is baptized shall be saved; but he that believeth not shall be damned." **(Mark 16:15-16)**

Again we see that the gospel is first to be preached; then those who believe and are baptized will be saved. Believe in what? The gospel, which is the message of the death, burial and resurrection of Jesus Christ.

When we put these scriptures together, we see that a person must first have a repentant heart, turning from evil ways, and then turning to God through believing in Jesus Christ and His finished work on the cross. As scripture tells us, if we do these things we shall be saved.

When we are baptized as Christians, it is a time when we can release our faith toward God, acknowledging that these changes have really taken place in our lives. It is a specific point in time when we can confess publicly these changes have taken place and we are committing ourselves to walk in them by faith - to leave the old nature (man) in the watery grave and allow the new nature (man) to reign victorious in our lives. This decision, once it has been made, is the beginning of the renewing of our minds in Christ.

The minute we receive Christ, our hearts are changed (we are born again), but there is a war that still rages on in our minds. Our minds therefore need to be renewed (changed) - **2 Corinthians 10:3-5** explains this. *"For though we walk in the flesh, we do not war according to the flesh. For the weapons of our warfare are not carnal but mighty in God for pulling down strongholds, casting down arguments and every high thing that exalts itself against the knowledge of God, bringing every thought into captivity to the obedience of Christ."*

There is often a real point of victory (release) at the time of water baptism just as we saw the enemies of Israel destroyed as they crossed through the Red Sea. Our part in water baptism is to acknowledge by faith that Jesus has destroyed that old nature and He has established us to walk in our new nature. **NOTE:** For examples of people who were baptized see **Acts 2:38, 8:16, 10:48, 19:5.**

Holy Spirit Baptism

"But you will receive power when the Holy Spirit comes on you and you shall be witnesses to Me in Jerusalem, and in Judea, and Samaria, and to all the ends of the earth. (Acts 1:8) The first question a Christian might ask is, "Why do I need the Holy Spirit Baptism in my life?" The answer lies in the above scripture that says we are to be witnesses in the world. Does this scripture tell us that we get more Holy Spirit if we share more? No, it tells us we will receive power from the Holy Spirit that will give us the boldness to proclaim the gospel to all nations. It is by the strengthening and power of the Holy Spirit that we will accomplish all that God has for us. Those that God calls He also equips (empowers) to run the race that has been set before them.

When could the Holy Spirit come to live in us?

"But this spake He of the Spirit, which they that believe should receive: for the Holy Ghost was not yet given; because that Jesus was not yet glorified." (John 7:39) We are told that the Holy Spirit had not yet been given because Jesus had not yet been glorified. When was Jesus glorified? When He rose from the dead and returned to His Father in heaven.

When specifically did Jesus pour out His Spirit. *"And when the day of Pentecost was fully come, they were all with one accord in one place. And suddenly there came a sound from heaven as of a rushing mighty wind, and it filled all the house where they were sitting. And there appeared unto them cloven tongues like as of fire, and it sat upon each of them. And they were all filled with the Holy Ghost, and began to speak with tongues, as the Spirit gave them utterance."* **(Acts 2:1-4)**

If you remember as we studied the baptism of John, John makes a statement in **Matthew 3:11**, *"The one coming after him (Jesus) would baptize with the Holy Spirit and fire."* The time had come, God poured out his Spirit upon his people on the day of Pentecost.

What was the evidence of the baptism of the Holy Spirit? Verse 4 tells us that they spoke in other tongues as the Spirit gave them utterance. As you continue to read Chapter 2 of the book of Acts, you will see that after receiving the baptism of the Holy Spirit, the disciples went out boldly - proclaiming the gospel and over 3000 people were saved on that day alone.

Without the working of the Holy Spirit this would have been impossible. Often Christians are zealous to serve God, but without the working of the Holy Spirit in their lives, they will have little or no results in their witnessing and will soon burn themselves out with many heartaches and disappointments. The Holy Spirit will give us supernatural abilities and the strength to accomplish the tasks God has given us to do. We will no longer have to rely on our own limited strength.

"Now when this noise occurred, the multitude came together, and were confounded, because they heard every man speaking in his own language. Then they were all amazed and marveled, saying one to another, 'Behold, are not all these which speak Galileans? And how hear we every man in our own tongue, in which we were born? Cretes and Arabians, we do hear them speak in our tongues the wonderful works of God.'" **(Acts 2:6-8,11)**

As we read this account we see that the multitudes heard the disciples speaking in other languages and as they listened they could understand one another. What did they hear? Verse 11 tells us they were hearing the wonderful works of God (the gospel). This is referred to in scripture as the gift of tongues (see **I Corinthians 12:1-12)**. The gift of tongues is the supernatural ability to speak in a language that has never been learned by the speaker, but yet is understood by those listening.

I have heard many testimonies of missionaries who have experienced this gift from God in their lives where it would have been impossible to share the gospel, God makes a way with this gift. God distributes His gifts in the body of Christ according to His will. The gift of tongues is not in the scope of this study but is mentioned so that there would be no confusion between the gift of tongues and the Holy Spirit prayer language that is available to all believers.

"But you beloved, building yourselves up on your most holy faith, praying in the Holy Spirit." **(Jude 20)** Here we are clearly told that as we pray in the Holy Spirit our faith will be built up or will grow. What is praying in the Holy Spirit? First we need to ask, what is prayer? Prayer is literally talking to God. Praying in the Holy Spirit is talking to God in a language that is unknown to the person praying but known to God.

Why would we want to pray to God in a language that is unknown to us and to anyone else? *"For he who speaks in a tongue does not speak to men but to God, for no one understands him; however in the Spirit, he speaks mysteries."* **(1 Corinthians 14:2)** *"Likewise the Spirit also helps us in our weakness. For we do not know what we should pray for as we ought, but the Spirit Himself makes intercession for us with groanings which cannot be uttered. Now He who searches the hearts knows what the mind of the Spirit is, because He makes intercession for the saints according to the will of God."* **(Romans 8:26-27)**

One of the biggest hindrances to praying to God is our own mind. What I mean is our own emotions and ideas that are contrary to God's plans interfere in our prayer lives. Thus after a period of time, because we are not praying according to the will of God, our prayer lives become dry and unfruitful. This is where the ministry of the Holy Spirit can be relied upon. When we really do not know the will of God in a situation we can pray in the Spirit. Since God's Spirit is within us, working directly with our spirit, pure and perfect prayer will be going up before the Father in heaven.

As we pray according to the will of God things will happen for God watches over His Word (which is His will) to see that it performs in the way He desires (see **Isaiah 55:11**). We see in the above scripture that the Holy Spirit even intercedes on our behalf. When we don't have the answer; when we are on the bottom looking up; we can rely on the Holy Spirit working on our behalf knowing our heart and making it known to our heavenly Father above who loves us and will move on our behalf.

In summary why do we speak in tongues?

A) We have the gift of tongues to proclaim the gospel to a person(s) in a language we do not know.
B) To build up our personal faith through the Holy Spirit interceding on our behalf.
C) To build up our prayer in God's will. (pure, perfect prayers).

HOW TO RECEIVE THE BAPTISM OF THE HOLY SPIRIT

The first qualification to receive the baptism or the empowering of the Holy Spirit is to be a believer. If you have not received Jesus into your heart the Holy Spirit does not live within you. How can you be empowered with something that is not in you? This is the reason why the world cannot accept the Holy Spirit. They can neither see Him nor understand Him. But as believers, we do know the Holy Spirit and understand Him for He lives inside of us. Since Jesus is now in heaven the Holy Spirit is immediately available to everyone who confesses Jesus as Lord. ***"Then Peter said unto them, Repent, and be baptized every one of you in the name of Jesus Christ for the remission of sins, and ye shall receive the gift of the Holy Ghost."*** (Acts 2:38)

Another qualification to receive the baptism of the Holy Spirit is to have a repentant heart. To understand this we have to look at the purpose and ministry of the Holy Spirit. The Holy Spirit lives in us to empower us, teach us, counsel, and direct us. In other words, to help us because we are not perfect. To have a repentant heart to the Holy Spirit means to submit to His working in us. When our opinion does not line up with God's verdict, we must choose God's judgement over ours. This is having a repentant heart. When we are baptized in the Holy Spirit with the evidence of speaking in tongues, we are in complete submission to God, allowing our voice box and tongue to be a direct extension of the Spirit of God in us.

To receive the baptism of the Holy Spirit we must be hungering after God. ***"In the last day, that great day of the feast, Jesus stood and cried, saying, 'If any man thirst, let Him come unto Me, and drink. He that believeth on Me, as the scripture hath said, out of his belly shall flow rivers of living water.'"*** (John 7:37-38)

As we thirst after God, acknowledging that He is the giver of all good things, what will happen? Out of our heart (inner most being) shall flow rivers of living water. Who lives in our hearts? The Holy Spirit lives in our hearts and from that Holy Spirit will come these living waters. A part of these living waters is the ability to speak in an unknown tongue. Another is the gifts of the Holy Spirit that God has reserved for us, and a third is a boldness to proclaim the Gospel. As you read these points, you can see that as we hunger after God and His power flows into us, the Holy Spirit and His power will then flow out of us to affect the people and the world around us.

Finally, we must have the faith to receive the promise of the Holy Spirit. ***"That the blessing of Abraham might come on the Gentiles through Jesus Christ; that we might receive the*** *promise of the Spirit through faith."* **(Galatians 3:14)** What is faith? Faith is believing or trusting that God's Word is true and then applying those truths to your life. This is real faith. Often false teaching or false doctrine can hinder a person from receiving the Holy Spirit baptism.

For example, if a person is taught that speaking in tongues is not for all believers this could be a stumbling block, for if the person has only a little faith to believe it challenges the integrity or truth of God's Word. Thus, it nullifies their faith in one of God's most precious promises, the baptism of the Holy Spirit. Thank God that through correct teaching and understanding of the Word of God, faith can be built up in a believer's life to a point of receiving and welcoming the baptism of the Holy Spirit. Also through the laying on of hands (which we will study in the next section), faith can be imparted from other believers to overcome unbelief that the baptism of the Holy Spirit will become manifest in that believer's life, to the glory and praise of God our Creator who loves us and wants the best for each of us.

To understand more fully the difference of operating without, and then in the fullness of the baptism of the Holy Spirit, we will look at the life of Peter. *"Peter said unto him, 'Lord, why cannot I follow thee now? I will lay down my life for thy sake.' Jesus answered him, "Wilt thou lay down thy life for My sake? Verily, verily, I say unto thee, the cock shall not crow, till thou hast denied Me thrice."* **(John 13:37-38)**

We see Peter telling Jesus that he would lay down his own life for Jesus, yet Jesus makes it clear that Peter is really not able to do this. Why not? Is it because Peter really was not committed? Peter had left his business, his wife, and all he had to follow Jesus for three and a half years. I believe that commitment was not the problem.

The key to the real answer is found in the Gospel of Matthew, where Jesus is speaking to Peter in the garden of Gethsemane before his arrest. *"And he cometh unto the disciples, and findeth them asleep, and saith unto Peter, 'What, could ye not watch with Me one hour? Watch and pray, that ye enter not into temptation: the spirit indeed is willing, but the flesh is weak.'"* **(Matthew 26: 40-41)**

The key is Jesus telling Peter that his spirit is willing but the flesh is weak. Later, when Peter is put to the test just as Jesus predicted, he denied Him three times. Why did Peter fail at this point in his life? When a person receives the baptism of the Holy Spirit, one of the most influential parts of our physical bodies should be yielded to the Holy Spirit - the tongue. It was through Peter's mouth that he denied Jesus. Peter did not want to deny his Lord, but his physical being overcame what his own spirit wanted to do. Fear of persecution and even the thought of death kept him from doing the right thing. The baptism of the Holy Spirit enables us to have a supernatural ability to rule over our minds and bodies.

What happened to Peter after he received the Holy Spirit Baptism? *"But Peter, standing up with the eleven, lifted up his voice, and said unto them, 'ye men of Judea, and all ye that dwell at Jerusalem, be this known unto you, and hearken to my words.'"* **(Acts 2:14)** This scripture occurs after Peter was baptized in the Holy Spirit and we see a new man. Peter boldly stands up before the same people he ran away from earlier and proclaims the gospel to them. The fruit of this is found in verse 41 of Acts 2 where we see 3000 people receiving Jesus through this first sermon of Peter. Don't we all want to be like this Peter, filled with the Holy Spirit not afraid, but bold to share the love of Jesus with those who are lost and in need of a Savior?

The baptism of the Holy Spirit is a supernatural empowering released by faith so that we may be confident to accomplish all that God has called us to do. It is a wonderful thing to know that the baptism of the Holy Spirit is available to all believers to empower them to perform and complete the calling that God has put on their lives.

Baptism of Suffering

This scripture clearly points to the fact that we as believers will suffer; it is unavoidable. **"*In fact everyone who wants to live a godly life will be persecuted (suffer).*"** **(2 Timothy 3:12)** One concept or truth many Christians do not understand is that there are some things we do not have to suffer, as we will see later in our study. Many modern theologians refer to the baptism of suffering as the baptism of maturity.

WHAT DO WE HAVE TO SUFFER FOR AS A CHRISTIAN?
A.) We as Christians will suffer for well doing

"For it is better, if the will of God be so, that ye suffer for well doing, than for evil doing." **(1 Peter 3:17)**

"For what glory is it, if, when ye be buffeted for your faults, ye shall take it patiently? But if, when ye do well, and suffer for it, ye take it patiently, this is acceptable with God." **(1 Peter 2:20)**

As we study the above scriptures we can see suffering in two different lights. Firstly, we are told that if we do wrong and suffer for it that is of no value to us, but if we suffer for doing right that is acceptable in God's sight. We are new creations in Jesus. If we suffer for doing something wrong how could that be considered acceptable to our heavenly Father? On the other hand, if we are persecuted for well doing at our own cost, we are an example to the world of the extent of the love of God. Therefore, we as Christians are to suffer for well doing.

B.) We as Christians are to suffer persecution

The people of the world have a desire to satisfy their own selfish ambitions, to satisfy the lusts of the flesh. We as Christians will suffer persecution because of our desire to live godly lives. *"Yes, and all who desire to live godly in Christ Jesus will suffer persecution."* **(2 Timothy 3:12)** We as Spirit-filled, born again believers are no longer going in that same downward current; we are headed upward against the flow, going against the pattern of this world. Our desire is to see God work in our lives to His honor and glory. Now, for us who are believers, it is a wonderful thing to seek God's purpose, going against the ways of the world (which are opposite God's ways). The problem that arises is when we bump into the people going downstream as we are headed upstream. First come the curious questions. Then, after the people of the world can't influence our stand for Jesus, they persecute us. We will suffer persecution.

C.) We as Christians will suffer temptation

Before we come to an understanding of what it is to suffer temptation, we first must understand the meaning of temptation. Temptation is a thought or desire that if acted upon would draw us away from the plans and purposes that God has for each of us. *"There hath no temptation taken you but such is common to man: but God is faithful, who will not suffer you to be tempted above that ye are able; but will with the temptation also make a way to escape, that ye may be able to bear it."* **(1 Corinthians 10:13)**

We will all suffer temptation for that is common to man. We as Christians must remember that temptations become sin only when a temptation is meditated upon and actions follow; we then cross the line into sin. The best thing to do when tempted is to do what Jesus did (see **Luke 4**). When the devil tempted Jesus, He always answered with "thus saith the Lord," and quoted scripture. We as followers of Christ must learn to overcome temptations by using the Word of God.

WHAT DO WE <u>NOT</u> HAVE TO SUFFER AS A CHRISTIAN?
A.) We do not have to suffer for our sins in eternity

Jesus died on the cross in our place, so we would not have to pay the penalty for our sins. *"Jesus was turned over to death for our sins and raised to life for our justification. Therefore, having been justified by faith, we have peace with God through our Lord Jesus Christ."* **(Rom:4:25-5:1)**
As we by faith acknowledge this truth, we are restored back into fellowship with God. No longer do we have to worry about suffering or paying the price for our sins. Jesus Christ has paid the price for us and our future is secure in Jesus Christ. For further reading on this topic see **Isaiah 53.**

B.) We do not have to suffer sickness

Part of the price that Jesus paid for us at Calvary is that He has already healed us from sickness. *"Who His own self bare our sins in His own body on the tree that we, being dead to sins, should live unto righteousness: by whose stripes ye were healed."* **(1 Peter 2:24)** Many Christians who are sick question the truth of this doctrine. The biggest mistake we can make is to take the Word of God and change or alter it to fit our experience. Rather, we need to take our experience and line it up with the absolute truth of God's word.

There are many factors that would hinder a person from being healed - for example, disobedience. How could a believer expect to be healthy if he is not in God's will? If I explained to my 10-year-old not to play on the street and he got hurt from an oncoming car, does my 10-year-old have any right to blame me? No, but like any good parent I would reach out to help so that his health would be restored. God wants to help us as well. God's Word tells us that God wants to protect and keep us just as a "hen would gather and protect her chicks." Jesus paid the price to remove sickness from us. Healing is for today!

C.) We do not have to suffer poverty

Jesus Christ, who is God, became man leaving all His heavenly splendor. *"For you know the grace of our Lord Jesus Christ, that though He was rich, yet for your sakes He became poor, that you through His poverty might become rich."* **(2 Corinthians 8:9)** Imagine the Creator of the universe becoming a man in every way yet He was without sin.

Jesus Christ completely emptied Himself on the cross of all the riches of heaven to restore us back into a relationship to God through Himself. Therefore, we can be called heirs of God and joint heirs of Christ; we now have an inheritance from God, our new Father. Even though we may not receive the fullness of this inheritance from heaven until we die, we are promised that all of our needs will be met in Christ Jesus here and now on this earth. We therefore have no need to suffer poverty because Jesus suffered on our behalf.

D.) We do not have to suffer as a murderer, thief, evildoer or meddler

"But let none of you suffer as a murderer, a thief, an evildoer, or as a busybody in other people's matters." **(1 Peter 4:15)**

Why should none of us suffer for the things listed in the above scripture? All of these things are what we would do as children of darkness. As born again Christians we are new creatures in Christ. We are no longer to follow the patterns of the world but we are to follow the example given to us by Jesus. If we perform any of the activities listed in this scripture, we should suffer.

But suffering for the above actions will not bring honor and glory to Jesus in any way; but rather will bring reproach and shame upon Him. We are to walk in the new nature that has been given us so that we will not fall into these sinful activities. Jesus suffered and died a criminal's death on the cross so we would not have to suffer for these things. Before we knew Jesus, we performed many of these actions at various times in our life and deserve punishment. But Jesus has paid the penalty for us.

SUMMARY OF SUFFERING

When we suffer for the name of Jesus we are to rejoice. Does this mean that we are to look forward to suffering? *"But rejoice to the extent that you partake of Christ's suffering, that when His glory is revealed, you may be glad with exceeding joy."* **(1 Peter 4:13)** When suffering for Jesus we can look past the time of suffering to the reward that we will receive in eternity.

"Looking unto Jesus the author and finisher of our faith; who for the joy that was set before him endured the cross, despising the shame, and is set down at the right hand of the throne of God." **(Hebrews 12:2)**

We know from the garden of Gethsemane that Jesus did not want to suffer and die on the cross, yet the above scripture tells of the "joy that was set before Him to endure the cross." That joy was not the crucifixion, but rather the results of the crucifixion. As Jesus suffered and died on the cross, he was looking ahead to you and me, knowing that through His suffering we were brought back into fellowship with our Creator.

We should arm ourselves with the same attitude; that when we suffer for Jesus and rejoice, we are being a living testimony of the love of God and an example to the world of the sure hope of eternal life with Jesus. As we walk through this life going through the baptism of maturity (baptism of suffering), the love of God continues to grow on the inside of us so that we can even shine brighter as a beacon of hope to the world for Jesus' sake. As a Christian, are you suffering for the right things? Examine your life in the light of what you now know.

STUDY QUESTIONS (LESSON 3 - DOCTRINE OF BAPTISMS)

1. What are the four types of baptisms that we have studied?_____
_____
_____
_____

2. What was the purpose of John's baptism?_____
_____

3. Can you give at least five reasons why a Christian should be baptized?_____
_____
_____
_____

4. What are two main reasons why infants are not eligible for baptism?_____
_____
_____

5. What conditions must be met to receive the baptism of the Holy Spirit?_____
_____
_____

6. Name some of the changes that Peter experienced in his life after he received the baptism of the Holy Spirit?_____
_____
_____

7. What is the most important thing that Jesus suffered for us?_____
_____

8. When we suffer for the name of Christ, how are we to react?_____
_____
_____

9. Have you been adult water baptized _____and baptized in the Holy Spirit?_____

10. Do you have to be water baptized and baptized in the Holy Spirit to be saved? Explain. _____
_____
_____

NOTES

CHAPTER 4: THE DOCTRINE OF LAYING ON OF HANDS

"Therefore, leaving the discussion of the elementary principles of Christ, let us go on to perfection, not laying again the foundation of repentance from dead works and of faith toward God, ² of the doctrine of baptisms, of laying on of hands, of resurrection of the dead, and of eternal judgment." **(Hebrews 6:1-2)**

Why do we have the foundational doctrine of laying on of hands in the church today? Can any believer in Jesus exercise this doctrine in their lives? The laying on of hands has been interpreted as something that only elders and church leaders can use. We will see in this study that the laying on of hands is for all believers to use in the extension of the Kingdom of God. If this were not true, the laying on of hands would not be one of the foundational doctrines.

NOTE: Always remember that the laying on of hands is a point of contact between two or more people to release faith.

There are five areas or reasons given to us in scripture to show the outworking of the doctrine of laying on of hands:

1) Blessings
2) Healing
3) Receive baptism in the Holy Spirit
4) Receive spiritual gifts
5) Commission Ministers

1) The Laying on of Hands for Blessing

The word *bless* simply means to speak well of, to praise, and to invoke a benediction upon. In the Old Testament there is a wonderful account of the laying on of hands for blessing.

"And Israel beheld Joseph's sons, and said, "who are these?" And Joseph said unto his father, "They are my sons, whom God hath given me in this place." And he said, "Bring them, I pray thee, unto me and I will bless them." Now the eyes of Israel were dim for age, so that he could not see. And he brought them near unto him; and he kissed them, and embraced them. And Israel said unto Joseph, "I had not thought to see thy face: and, lo, God hath

shown me also thy seed." And Joseph brought them out from between his knees, and he bowed himself with his face to the earth. And Joseph took them both, Ephraim in his right hand towards Israel's left hand, and Manasseh in his left hand toward Israel's right hand, and brought them near unto them. And Israel stretched out his right hand, and laid it upon Ephraim's head, guiding his hands knowingly; for Manasseh was the firstborn.

And he blessed Joseph and said, "God, before whom my fathers Abraham and Isaac did walk, the God which fed me all my life unto this day, the angel which redeemed me from all evil, bless the lads; and let my name be named on them, and the name of my fathers Abraham and Isaac; and let them grow into a multitude in the midst of the earth." And when Joseph saw that his father laid his right hand upon the head of Ephraim, it displeased him: and he held up his father's hand to remove it from Ephraim's head unto Manasseh's head.

And Joseph said unto his father, "Not so, my father: for this is the firstborn; put thy right hand upon his head." And his father refused, and said, "I know it, my son, I know it: he also shall become a people, and he also shall be great: but truly his younger brother shall be greater than he, and his seed shall become a multitude of nations." And he blessed them that day, saying, In thee shall Israel bless, saying, "God make thee as Ephraim and Manasseh: and he set Ephraim before Manasseh." **(Genesis 48:8-20)**

As we read this account we see that the doctrine of laying on of hands should not be taken lightly, as true blessings do not come from man but originate with God. At the end of Israel's (Jacob's) life, he blesses his two grandsons, the sons of Joseph. Israel placed his right hand on the younger son, Ephraim, indicating he would become greater than Manasseh, the elder brother.

This was completely contrary to tradition which always said the oldest son would receive the greatest blessing. However, Israel was not speaking his own will over the boys but rather God's will, which is often contrary to what we think is best (see Verse 17-18 to see how Joseph felt). The laying on of hands for blessing is a supernatural work of God.

There are no age restrictions concerning who we can lay hands upon. *"And Jesus took the children in His arms, put his hands on them and blessed them."* **(Mark 10:16)** As spiritual leaders in our households we should exercise the laying on of hands for blessings. God spoke and at His Word, the universe was created. Likewise, we are created in the image of God; therefore, as sons of God our words have power as well. There are only two ways our words can have an effect; either for blessing or for cursing. The Word clearly tells us that we are no longer to curse as we did in our former lives. This means that our words are to be used to bless. Reflect for a moment on your children and other loved ones who are confronted with the world on a daily basis.

Now consider all the negative words or curses that have been or may be spoken against them. In the name and power of Jesus we can come against these curses through the laying on of hands to invoke blessings to overcome those curses. These blessings can and will have an effect for a lifetime onto eternity. One practical example to share came from a Foundations class that I was teaching. A student named Sally, who is a teacher in a public school, explained how she was often overwhelmed by certain students because of their behavior. As she related further details of these students' lives, we both realized that the problem students came from broken homes or homes which were in turmoil.

Often these students caused all sorts of problems and disruptions both for themselves and for their classmates. I suggested that Sally should practice the laying on of hands. Sally began walking the aisles of her classroom monitoring the progress of her students. She would rest her hands on the shoulders of the problem students as if to be checking their school work.

Unbeknownst to the student, Sally would pray quietly in the Spirit to herself over each of these children. The results were astounding. Sally came back to class the next week and shared how these previously disruptive children had miraculously been affected, evidenced by dramatically improved behavior. The only thing she could attribute this change to was the laying on of hands and by praying in the Spirit.

2) The Laying on of Hands for Healing

"And He (Jesus) said to them, "Go into all the world and preach the gospel to every creature. He who believes and is baptized will be saved, but he who does not believe will be condemned. And these signs will follow those who believe: In My name they will cast out demons; they will speak with new tongues; they will take up serpents; and if they drink anything deadly, it will by no means hurt them; they will LAY HANDS ON THE SICK, AND THEY WILL RECOVER." **(Mark 16:15-18)**

NOTE: The laying on of hands for the healing of the sick is only one of five supernatural signs listed in this scripture. Notice that the entire purpose of all of these signs was that through the tangible demonstration of the power of God people might believe and be saved.

The aforementioned scripture is often referred to as the Great Commission. The last portion speaks of laying hands on sick people and the sick recovering. According to this scripture, the only qualification we need to lay hands on the sick is to be a believer; in other words, to be born again.

The healing of the sick has been a controversial issue in Christian circles. Some say that the healing gifts ended when the apostles died. Others speak of God's inability to heal until we receive our new bodies. Why are there so many varying opinions on the laying on of hands for healing today? Many Christians develop opinions after they have laid hands on someone to be healed and the healing is not manifested. These individuals therefore conclude that they will rely upon and trust in their own failed experience rather than to exercise faith in the Word of God.

Christians who fall prey to this mode of thinking are being deceived by the lies of the devil. Is it not human nature that when something does not work we blame the other person or party involved rather than ourselves? When these people say that "healing is not for today," in effect they are calling God a liar. Since we **know** that God is not a liar, let us trust His word and not give up.

In **Mark 16:15-18**, the word **"believe"** is mentioned several times. An alternate translation to this word is **"to trust."** The ability to trust someone implies having an intimate relationship or a closeness to that person. This scripture discusses trusting in God; having an intimate relationship or closeness of relationship with God. To operate in the supernatural and see the hand of God move, we must be submitted to the voice of the Holy Spirit that lives on the inside of us. We must lay down our own will and submit to the Father's will.

A good example of a healing is found in chapter five of the Gospel of John. Here we see Jesus coming to the pool of Bethesda at Jerusalem. At this place the Bible tells us that multitudes of sick people stayed, hoping to be healed by the moving of the waters.

Many were blind, lame or paralyzed. Tradition said that at a certain time an angel would come down from heaven and stir the waters.

The first one to get into the waters after they were stirred would be healed from their infirmity. Now Jesus came onto this scene and focused on one man.

Knowing that this man had been in a bed-stricken condition for 38 years, Jesus asked him if he would like to be healed. The man answered yes, explaining the fact that he was looking to the water for his healing. In verse eight, Jesus told the man to rise, take up his bed and walk. This man, acting by faith (trusting in what Jesus had said), rose up and was totally healed.

Many people have difficulty understanding this account of healing because only one man was healed. What about the multitude of others who needed to be healed? A clue to the answer of this question is found in verse 19. *"Then Jesus answered and said to them," Most assuredly I say to you, the Son of Man can do nothing of Himself, but what He sees the Father do; for whatever He does, the Son also does in like manner."* **(John 5:19)**

Jesus said that He can do nothing of Himself but does only as he sees His Father do. In other words, Jesus did not do what He felt best to do, but rather did exactly as His Father in heaven told Him to do. Now you still may be asking the question, "What about the others needing healing; does this mean that God shows favoritism?" To answer this question, we must once again look at the healing of the paralytic at the pool. Do you think that this man, when healed after being a paralytic for 38 years, silently and unobtrusively departed from the area?

I can most assuredly tell you that he praised God in a very loud voice when this miracle happened in his life. What do you imagine might be the response of the multitudes around the pool? **John 5:3-4,** tells us that the people were looking to the mysterious moving of the water for their healing.

Again the sick multitudes were looking to this pool of water as their ticket to health, rather than looking to the Great Physician, Jesus Christ the Son of God, who not only could heal them of their physical infirmities, but save them from their sins as well. If anyone of the multitudes had come to Jesus by faith, they would have been healed. In every healing account in scripture, Jesus healed EVERYONE who came to Him and none were turned away.

"Then Jesus went out from there and came to His own country, and His disciples followed Him. And when the Sabbath had come He began to teach in the synagogue. And many hearing Him were astonished saying, "Where did this Man get these things? And what

wisdom is this which is given to Him, that such mighty works are performed by His hands! Is this not the carpenter, the Son of Mary, and the brother of James, Joses, Judas, and Simon? And are not His sisters here with us?"

And they were offended at Him. But Jesus said to them, "A prophet is not without honor except in his own country, among his own relatives and in his own house." Now He could do no mighty works there except that He LAID HIS HANDS ON A FEW SICK PEOPLE AND HEALED THEM. And He marveled at their unbelief. Then Jesus went about the villages in a circuit, teaching." **(Mark 6:1-6)**

What made this particular village different from the others where Jesus had taught with great signs and wonders? First, we must see that this was the hometown of Jesus, where he had been brought up. The people only acknowledged what they had seen when Jesus had lived there, as a carpenter's son.

So we see Jesus was amazed at their unbelief and could only perform a few miracles through the laying on of hands. In other places in the Bible we can see that Jesus would often just speak a word to a sick person, and the sick person acting by faith would rise up out of their sickness. It was the combination of the Word of God and their own personal faith in that spoken word that brought about their healing. But in Jesus' hometown, no one had any faith in Jesus. Yet there was a way that Jesus knew He could overcome their unbelief. This was through the laying on of hands.

By the physical laying on of hands Jesus spoke the Word and through His own faith healed the people. We can take also this principle one step further. If a believer comes to us to unite in prayer for healing and we know the Word of God states that "Each of us has been given a measure of faith," (Romans 12:3), we can then lay hands on them and speak the Word of God. The coupling of our faith with theirs will produce astounding results, for God's Word will never fail. **Hebrews 11:6** tells us that it pleases God for us to come to Him by faith, and we will be rewarded for diligently seeking Him.

"Now Jesus was teaching in one of the synagogues on the Sabbath. And behold there was a woman who had a spirit of infirmity 18 years, and was bent over and could in no way raise herself up. But when Jesus saw her, He called her to Him and said to her, "Woman you are loosed from your infirmity." And HE LAID HANDS ON HER, and immediately she was

made straight, and glorified God. But the ruler of the synagogue answered with indignation, because Jesus had healed on the Sabbath; and he said to the crowd, "There are six days in which men ought to work; therefore come and be healed on them and not on the Sabbath day." The Lord then answered him and said, "Hypocrite! Does not each one of you on the Sabbath loose his ox or donkey from the stall and lead it away to water it? So ought not this woman, being a daughter of Abraham, whom satan has bound (think of it) for 18 years, be loosed from this bondage on the Sabbath." **(Luke 13:10-16)**

In this particular healing there were demonic forces directly involved with this woman's infirmity. What we see is Jesus speaking forth a word and then, through the laying on of hands, the woman was loosed from her infirmity. Verse 16 tells us Satan had kept this woman BOUND but that she had been LOOSED (set free) from the evil spirit. Just as Jesus was sent into the world to set the captives free, our job is to continue His work by doing just that, setting the captives free. As we have just read, the healing of a person may involve the deliverance from demonic forces in that person's life.

The healing will only be permanent when the healed person fills the void left by the evil spirit with the Word of God and the Spirit of God. In this way, if the demonic force returns and tries to take up residency in that person's life again, there will be no place for it to live. Again, we see the laying on of hands as a powerful tool in the extension of the Kingdom of God.

"Now in that region there was an estate of the leading citizen of the island, whose name was Publius, who received us and entertained us courteously for three days. And it happened that the father of Publius lay sick of a fever and dysentery and Paul went into him and prayed, and HE LAID HIS HANDS ON HIM AND HEALED HIM. So when this was done, the rest of those on the Island who had diseases also came and were healed." **(Acts 28:7-9)**

It was a man named Paul whom God worked through to perform these healings. Many people believe the lie that the gift of laying on of hands for healing ceased to operate after all the original apostles died. Please take note that Paul was not one of the original twelve and in fact was not even born again for a number of years after the death and resurrection of Jesus. Yet we see this man operating freely in this gift. Notice the outcome of Publius' father being healed; all of the rest of the people who had a need came and were healed. You can be sure that Paul shared the Gospel of Jesus with these people, and many believed because of the miracles that occurred.

In the Gospel of **Mark 16:18**, we are told to lay hands on the sick and they will recover. This scripture is part of the Great Commission that Jesus gave to ALL BELIEVERS to perform. Do we need any more evidence to prove that God wants us to use the laying on of hands for healing today?

3) The Laying on of Hands for Baptism in the Holy Spirit

"He who believes in Me (Jesus), as scripture has said, out of his heart shall flow rivers of living water. But this He (Jesus) spoke concerning the Spirit, whom those believing in Him would receive; for the Holy Spirit was not yet given, because Jesus was not yet glorified." (John 7:38-39)

Jesus makes several clear points concerning the Holy Spirit. We see that the Holy Spirit is to be given to all believers. The Holy Spirit must live in our hearts, for He shall flow from our heart as rivers of living waters. We also see from this scripture that the Holy Spirit could not be given until Jesus was glorified. When was Jesus glorified? When Jesus came to this earth, He laid down His glory in heaven and became like man.

When Jesus was crucified and three days later was raised from the dead, the Bible tells us that after spending time with His disciples, He returned to heaven and received the former glory that He had. For further reading see **John chapters 15-17** concerning the glorification of Jesus and the coming of the Holy Spirit. For our study we need to know that the Holy Spirit is now available to any believer who by faith will allow Him to flow through him as the scripture has said, as living water from the heart.

Why do we need the Baptism of the Holy Spirit?

"But you shall receive POWER when the Holy Spirit is come upon you; and you shall be witnesses to Me in Jerusalem, and in Judea and Samaria, and to the ends of the earth." (Acts 1:8)

This power in the original Greek language is "*dunamus*," and it is from this word that we derive the word dynamite. With the Holy Spirit, we have within us the explosive power of God. The same power that raised Jesus Christ from the dead is within us. So what are we to do with this power? We are to be witnesses of the love, forgiveness and acceptance of God; but in this particular scripture, take note of who we are to be witnesses to. Since Jesus is speaking, He is stating that we are to be witnesses to Him.

What Jesus is really saying is that with the power of the Holy Spirit within us, we are to go forth on this earth proving or being a witness to God that His Word works. As we do this, unsaved people will get saved, set free and sanctified as the power of God explodes in their lives.

When a person receives the Baptism of the Holy Spirit what is the evidence?

"And when Paul had laid hands on them, the Holy Spirit came upon them, and they spoke with tongues and prophesied." **(Acts 19:6)**

This is just one example from scripture, but as confirmed in other accounts as well, the one main evidence of receiving the baptism of the Holy Spirit is speaking in a language unknown to yourself. We have seen already that the Holy Spirit resides in our heart, and Jesus tells us in **Matthew 12:34** that it is out of the abundance of the heart that the mouth speaks.

"Now when the apostles who were at Jerusalem heard that Samaria had received the Word of God, they sent Peter and John to them, who when they had come down, prayed for them that they might receive the Holy Spirit. For as yet He had fallen upon none of them. They had only been baptized in the name of Jesus. Then they LAID HANDS ON THEM and they RECEIVED THE HOLY SPIRIT.

Now when Simon saw that through the laying on of the apostles hands the Holy Spirit was given , he offered them money, saying, "Give me this power also that anyone on whom I lay hands may receive the Holy Spirit." But Peter said to him, "Your money perish with you, because you thought the gift of God could be purchased with money." **(Acts 8:14-20)**

We see in this particular scripture that the Holy Spirit was received through the laying on of hands. This scripture brings up an important issue concerning spiritual gifts; in the fact that they are just that, gifts given by God to mankind. Here we see a new believer who wants to buy the gift of God for money. Most Christians today would never think of trying what Simon did, ... or would they?

They might not use money in an attempt to buy the anointing and gifting of the Holy Spirit, but they might use other shortcuts to try to operate in the power and gifting of the Holy Spirit. I have personally seen people hop from one meeting to another, hoping the anointing and power that the speaker is operating in would somehow rub off on them, rather than taking the time to cultivate a personal relationship with Jesus who is the Author and Giver of the gifts.

It is only through a personal relationship that we gain access to receive the calling and gifts specifically set aside for us before the foundations of the world. Many people have the mentality that the grass is always greener on the opposite side of the fence, rather than searching for and feeding on the revelation of the Word that God has provided for them and then acting upon it. However, we do need to remember that the laying on of hands has been a gift that is for all believers to operate in for the extension of the kingdom of God, as we have seen in **Mark 16**, the Great Commission.

Many times when I have laid hands on and prayed with individuals to receive the baptism of the Holy Spirit, I have observed them to be looking up in the air or to one side or the other. At this point I ask them what they are doing. Invariably, they tell me that they are looking for the Holy Spirit. That would be like searching all through your house for your car keys when they were in your pocket all the time.

When a person asks Jesus to come into his heart as Lord and Savior, that is exactly what happens. Jesus sends His representative the Holy Spirit to live inside you. This happens when you are born again. You may be asking "why do I seek the baptism of the Holy Spirit if we already have Him inside of us as soon as we receive our salvation?" This seeking indicates the desire for a higher, or deeper or more complete level of submission.

Man is a triune being having a spirit, soul (mind) and body. When the Holy Spirit comes to live inside us we receive a new spirit. At this point the Holy Spirit becomes almost like a prisoner within us not being able to express Himself. When a person is baptized in the Holy Spirit, this is the point in the believer's life when he or she not only submits their spirit man to the Holy Spirit, but their mind and body as well.

This is why speaking in tongues is an excellent proof. Think about it in this way - under normal circumstances it is our mind that controls our tongue which is an extension of our body. When we by faith give both our minds and our bodies over to God, the first thing the Holy Spirit is going to do is to express Himself in a tangible way, hence the speaking in tongues.

As we have already learned, the laying on of hands is needed at times when the faith of a believer is not strong enough. I have found that once a believer has the understanding that the Holy Spirit already resides within him, the baptism of the Holy Spirit with evidence of speaking in tongues soon follows. Do not let the lack of understanding or false teaching keep you from receiving the baptism of the Holy Spirit; experience all that God has for you, empowered fully by the Holy Spirit.

4) The Laying On of Hands for Spiritual Gifts

There is a natural progression from the baptism of the Holy Spirit to spiritual gifts, as spiritual gifts come from the Holy Spirit. Until a believer has allowed the full reign of the Spirit of God within his entire being, gifts of the Holy Spirit cannot be manifested.

"Do not neglect your gift, which was given you through a prophetic message when the body of elders laid their hands on you." (1 Timothy 4:14)

The apostle Paul is speaking to young Timothy, reminding him of a time when hands had been laid on him. To fully understand this scripture we need to understand the word "prophecy." *Prophecy* is a message given by God through a believer to encourage, warn or rebuke another person. Prophecy should not be a surprise (something new) to the one receiving the word, but rather should confirm what God has already spoken to them through the Holy Spirit within them.

What Paul is really saying is, 'Timothy, do not neglect the gift that you already have and was confirmed through the laying on of hands and a word from the Lord through the elders.' A good illustration to explain spiritual gifts is when you receive a present at a birthday. Have you ever received a present that is a box, within a box, within a box, and so on? Even though you may not know what is in the next box, it is in your possession. This is how it is in the spirit realm.

When we are born again we receive this giant gift. Under the first wrapping is Jesus and the forgiveness of sins and the indwelling Holy Spirit. Next, as we continue to grow and seek after the Lord, we open the next package by faith: the baptism of the Holy Spirit. Next comes spiritual gifts the Lord has picked for us.

One thing we must always understand is that while we receive this complete gift at salvation, how quickly we reach spiritual maturity depends completely on us. This is a very simplified illustration because all the principles of God have been given to us as free gifts. What we must do is accept the gifts (principles) in our lives and then apply them by faith.

"As His divine power (Holy Spirit) has given us all things that pertain to life and godliness, through the knowledge of Him (Jesus) who called us by glory and virtue by which we have been given to us exceedingly great and precious promises, that through these you may be partakers of the divine nature, having escaped the corruption that is in the world through lust." (2 Peter 1:3-4)

We see the proof in the Word of God showing us that our heavenly Father has given us everything that we need for this life through His Son, Jesus, who in turn has given us His Holy Spirit to empower us that we may appropriate the promises of God. The key to being partakers of the divine nature is the knowledge of Jesus and His Word.

A powerful example that occurred in my life was when I had been born again for about six months. I had been reading the Word of God concerning the baptism of the Holy Spirit. At the time I was attending a church that did not believe in the baptism of the Holy Spirit with the evidence of speaking in tongues. Yet, as I read in the Word, I saw time after time that the baptism of the Holy Spirit was for the New Testament church and I was a part of that church.

As I continued to search the Word and spend time in prayer, faith began to rise up within me. One day as I was at work meditating on the things of God, I felt this faith rising up within my spirit, and before I knew it I was praising God in an unknown language. How did this occur? As I grew in the knowledge of the baptism of the Holy Spirit, understanding that it is a promise given to all believers, faith started to rise up within me until it overcame my unbelief and the promise was manifested in my life. However, there may be times when we need the laying on of hands of a fellow believer to increase our faith to receive this precious promise from the Kingdom of God.

"For this reason I remind you to fan into flame the gift of God, which is in you through the laying on of my hands." (2 Timothy 1:6)

We see Paul again addressing Timothy, reminding him of the gift of God that had been confirmed through the laying on of hands. Notice the reason why Paul is concerned for Timothy. Timothy had not been operating in the gift given him and needed to rekindle the gift through operating in it. The entire reason I have brought this scripture to light is because the laying on of hands is a very powerful tool that the Lord has given for spiritual gifts. But once the gift(s) have been revealed, it is completely up to us to exercise what God has given us.

Do you know what your spiritual gifts are? You can be sure that if you are a child of God with the Holy Spirit indwelling, there are spiritual gifts that need to be unwrapped. Begin today to seek the face of God in prayer and in the Word to discover what He has in store for you. Once you know within your heart what God is saying, go to the eldership of your church and let them pray for you, that it may be confirmed through prophetic utterance the gift(s) within you. Then begin to exercise those gifts, bearing witness to God and to the world that His Spirit is working through you.

5) The Laying on of Hands to Commission Ministers

"Now in the church that was at Antioch there were certain prophets and teachers: Barnabas, Simeon who was called Niger, Lucius of Cyrene, Manaen who had been brought up with Herod the tetrarch, and Saul. As they ministered to the Lord and fasted, the Holy Spirit said, "Now separate to Me Saul and Barnabus for the work to which I have called them." Then having fasted and prayed, and laid hands on them, they sent them away." (Acts 13:1-3)

We must recognize that it is the Holy Spirit who calls believers to acts of service. Those who are performing the laying on of hands are just confirming what the Holy Spirit is saying. Please note the fasting and praying that was done before Barnabus and Paul were sent out. This scripture also shows us that it was the leadership who commissioned Barnabas and Saul.

"Do not be hasty in the laying on of hands, and do not share in the sins of others. Keep yourself pure." (1 Timothy 5:22) This scripture has often been quoted for the purposes of being careful about who to pray for because of the spiritual dangers that might be involved.

We **do** need to hear the leading of the Holy Spirit before we lay hands on and pray for anyone. If we do this, we can be sure that God will protect us from any dangers.

This particular scripture is in reference to commissioning ministers. In **1 Timothy 3:1-13**, the apostle Paul gives Timothy guidelines for selecting leaders in the church. Paul was cautioning Timothy against hastily commissioning ministers through the laying on of hands; for if he commissioned someone who was not qualified to be a leader, and that person did something contrary to sound doctrine, Timothy would be responsible (or in other words be a partaker of that man's sins) because he had given him a position of authority within the church.

For the believer in the church who is not in a position of leadership, the laying on of hands for the commissioning of ministers is not our duty. Those who perform the laying on of hands for this purpose and in this authority must take responsibility for their actions. Our responsibility in this area is to pray for our leadership so they will make quality decisions concerning the commissioning of ministers.

CONCLUSION TO THE LAYING ON OF HANDS

As we have seen, the laying on of hands serves many purposes in the body of Christ. We must always remember that it is the Holy Spirit working through us in the ministry of the laying on of hands. We are to be yielded vessels the Holy Spirit can flow through, reaching out with the Gospel of Jesus Christ. Just as we have seen in scripture, believers of any maturity in Christ led by the Holy Spirit can lay hands on people and expect them to be healed in the name of Jesus.

As we listen and obey the voice of the Holy Spirit, God will give us opportunities to lay hands on people to receive the baptism of the Holy Spirit and spiritual gifts. The laying on of hands for the commissioning of ministers is the job of the eldership and church leaders; they must assume responsibility for whom they commission.

Always remember that the laying on of hands is a point of contact in which to release faith into a person's life. Begin today the practice of laying on of hands to bless and heal your spouse and children that in turn, you might grow in faith toward God, as the Holy Spirit works through you.

STUDY QUESTIONS (LESSON 4 - THE LAYING ON OF HANDS)

1. Why do we lay hands on a person when praying for them?_____
_____

2.What are the five possible reasons that we would lay hands on a person? _____,
_____, _____,
_____, _____

3. Why should we exercise the gift of laying on of hands for the purpose of blessing?
_____
_____

4. According to **Mark 16:15-18,** what are the qualifications required to pray for the sick?
_____

5. In **Mark 6:1-4**, we see Jesus performed no miracles except to pray for a few sick people and cure them. Why did this happen and how did Jesus heal some that were there? _____
_____
_____

6. Explain why through the laying on of hands the baptism of the Holy Spirit can be received.
_____
_____
_____

7. In your own words, why do you think the devil would get upset when we exercise spiritual gifts as listed in **1 Corinthians 12:4-11?**
_____
_____

8. Explain God's part and our part in the ministry of laying on of hands.
_____
_____

9. What is the only area of laying on of hands that we should not practice if we are not in a position of leadership and why?_____
_____
_____

NOTES

CHAPTER 5: THE RESURRECTION OF THE DEAD

"Therefore, leaving the discussion of the elementary principles of Christ, let us go on to perfection, not laying again the foundation of repentance from dead works and of faith toward God, ² of the doctrine of baptisms, of laying on of hands, <u>of resurrection of the dead</u>, and of eternal judgment." **(Hebrews 6:1-2)**

As the apostle Paul is speaking to the Christians at Corinth, we learn that when our physical body dies, our soul (and spirit) goes to be with Jesus. ***"We are confident, yes, well pleased rather to be absent from the body is to be present with the Lord."*** **(2 Corinthians 5:8)**

This one scripture alone leads us to several key questions. Do we have to be born again to live forever? What happens to unbelievers when they die? Has the above scripture always been true? To be absent from the body means to be with Jesus even before Jesus died on the cross. God very clearly in his Word lays out the answers to these questions making the doctrine of the resurrection of the dead an exciting study because it is a part of God's end time plan, a plan in which we all play a part.

Definition: *Resurrection* - to cause to stand up, or to rise from sleep and from the dead.

1.) Spiritual Resurrection

To begin our study we must first understand that there is a spiritual RESURRECTION (awakening) from the dead. Jesus, when speaking to Nicodemus the Pharisee, explains to us this doctrine.

"I tell you the truth, no one can SEE the kingdom of God unless he is BORN AGAIN." "I tell you the truth no one can ENTER the kingdom of God unless he is BORN of WATER and the SPIRIT." "For God so loved the world that He gave His only begotten Son that whosoever BELIEVES in Him should not perish but have EVERLASTING LIFE." **(John 3:3,5,16)**

In order to see and enter the Kingdom of Heaven, we must be born again. We see from verse 16 that it is by faith in the Son of God that we have everlasting life. To be spiritually resurrected means to be born again through faith in the Son of God (Jesus Christ).

We also see that if a person does not believe, he will perish (live forever separated from God). Spiritual resurrection (being born again) is by far the most important decision that a person makes in this life, for on this decision **alone** hinges where you will spend all of eternity (forever with God or forever separated from God). *What decision have you made?*

2.) Where Did People Go When They Died Before the Cross (before the resurrection of Jesus Christ)?

Before Jesus came to live as a man, millions of people lived and died on this earth. We know that many of these people were looking forward to the coming of the Messiah (Jesus) but died before He came. These people (i.e., Noah) were righteous in their generation (see **Genesis 6:8-9**). In other words, they had done what God had required them to do in their generation.

We see the real heart of God and the fact he wants ALL people to be saved. *"God wants all men to be saved and come to a knowledge of the truth. For there is one God and one Mediator between God and men, the man Jesus Christ, who gave Himself as a ransom for all men - the testimony given in its proper time."* **(1 Timothy 2:4-7)** To be saved, we must acknowledge the fact that Jesus gave himself as a ransom for us (paid the price of our sins).

At the end of this verse, we see that this happened at a particular point in time, almost 2,000 years ago. Even though many people who lived before the coming of Jesus had a heart for God, Jesus had not yet died for their sins, so they could not go to be with God until the Mediator, Jesus Christ, had accomplished His work on the cross. What did God do with these people until Jesus came? And where did the unrighteous go as well?

The Parable Of The Rich Man And Lazarus

"There was a certain rich man who was clothed in purple and fine linen and lived in luxury every day. But there was a certain beggar named Lazarus, full of sores who was laid at his gate, desiring to be fed with the crumbs that fell from the rich man's table. Moreover the dogs came and licked his sores. So it was that the beggar died, and was carried by the angels to Abraham's bosom. The rich man also died and was buried. And being in torments in Hades, he lifted up his eyes and saw Abraham afar off, and Lazarus in his bosom.

Then he cried and said, "Father Abraham, have mercy upon me, and send Lazarus that he may dip the tip of his finger in water and cool my tongue; for I am tormented in this flame." But Abraham said, "Son, remember that in your lifetime you received your good things, and likewise Lazarus evil things; but now he is comforted and you are tormented. And besides all this, between us and you there is a great gulf fixed, so that those who want to pass from here to you cannot, nor can those from there pass to us."

Then the rich man said, "I beg you therefore, father, that you would send Lazarus to my father's house, for I have five brothers that he may testify to them, lest they also come to this place of torment." Abraham said to him, "They have Moses and the prophets; let them hear them. And he said to them, "No, father Abraham; but if one goes to them from the dead, they will repent." But Abraham said to him, "If they do not hear Moses and the prophets, neither will they be persuaded though one rise from the dead." (Luke 16:19-31)

As we read this parable we may get the impression that when rich people die they go to hell and poor people go to heaven. But note as we have studied the scriptures, we have found that it is not our social status that decides our future in eternity, but rather our motivations and actions concerning the Lord Jesus Christ and a changed heart through the power of God (being born again).

This parable gives us tremendous insight into the two places in which people went before the death and resurrection of Jesus. The one place is called Abraham's bosom (paradise), and is a place of comfort, rest and peace. The other place is referred to as hades (hell), and is a place of fire, heat and torment with no relief. There is also a great chasm or gulf between these places so that one could not travel from one place to the other. Another point is the fact that our soul (and spirit) have physical-type senses. This dispels the thinking that when you die you go into nothingness where you feel neither good things nor bad things.

"Then the thief said to Jesus, "Lord remember me when You come into Your Kingdom." And Jesus said to him, "Assuredly, I say to you, today you will be with Me in PARADISE." (Luke 23:42-43)

This one thief, as he hung on a cross, came to the realization that he was going into eternity. Because of his evil deeds and guilt, he knew that he was headed to a place of eternal punishment. He had heard about Jesus and knew that Jesus had not been crucified because of evil deeds, but that

He was the Son of God, the King of kings. This thief came to a place where he knew he needed Jesus. What was the answer Jesus gave as the thief reached out to Him by faith, realizing that his eternity depended on Jesus? Jesus tells him, "Today you will be with Me in Paradise." When the thief heard the reply of Jesus, a peace that passes all understanding rose up within him, and instead of fearful anticipation of eternity came an expectancy of abundant life after physical death.

"Jesus, when He again cried out in a loud voice, yielded up His Spirit. And behold, the veil of the temple was torn from top to bottom; and the earth quaked, and the rocks were split, and the graves were opened and many bodies of the saints who had fallen asleep were raised; and coming out of the graves after His resurrection, they went into the holy city and appeared to many." **(Matthew 27:50-53)**

This scripture points out that Jesus yielded up His Spirit, confirming that even until the last second He could have prevented His own death if He had chosen to. Therefore, not only did Jesus choose to go to the cross and suffer for our sins, but He also chose to stay on the cross and suffer on our behalf. What really happened immediately after the death of Jesus? We see that the veil in the temple was torn from the top to the bottom. This veil was actually a very thick curtain approximately 1-1/2' thick and 30' high. This veil separated the Holy Place from the Most Holy Place in the temple in Jerusalem.

Under the Old Mosaic Law only the High Priest, once a year, could enter this part of the temple. When he entered the Most Holy Place, he went as the representative of the people with the blood of innocent animals to atone for or cover over the sins of the people and himself, until such a time when the ultimate perfect sacrifice (the Messiah or Savior) would come and take away the sins of the people.

Jesus Christ was that Savior, and after His death He took His own shed blood and entered the Most Holy Place in Heaven and placed His own blood on the mercy seat, taking away the sins of the people who had put their faith in Him. Jesus then turned and tore the temple curtain that separated the Holy Place from the Most Holy Place (where the presence of God was); showing us that we were no longer separated from God because of our sin, but through the shed blood of Jesus we have free access to our Heavenly Father.

In **Ephesians 3:12**, we are told that in Christ and through faith in Him we may approach God with all freedom and confidence. In seeing what Jesus did after His death in the temple, we can understand that no one could go to heaven until Jesus had finished His plan of redemption for mankind. Many theologians believe that Jesus went to Paradise just as he told the thief. While he was there, He emptied it out and brought out all those souls who believed and looked forward to the coming of Jesus, and He gave them their resurrected bodies.

This explains the scripture verse reporting of the sightings of saints who had previously died, being seen alive after the resurrection of Jesus. When Jesus went up into heaven, these people made up the great cloud of witnesses that surrounded Him (see **Hebrews 12:1, Ephesians 4:8**). The souls of those who are in hell remain there until a time called the Great White Throne Judgment, which we will study in our next lesson.

3.) The Physical Resurrection of Christ

Please read: **Matthew 28:1-10, Mark 16:1-14, Luke 24:1-47, John 20:1-31**

All of the above scriptures give an account of the bodily resurrection of Jesus Christ. Many people in the past and present have tried to prove that Jesus was never raised from the dead. Yet here are four accurate recorded accounts of the resurrection of Jesus. Everything that Jesus said before He was crucified came to pass. In the Old Testament, which had been written long before the birth of Jesus, there are over 700 detailed predictions concerning the birth, life, death and resurrection of the Messiah. Jesus has fulfilled each one of these prophesies **perfectly in every detail.**

The most compelling evidence to convince us as believers of the resurrection of Christ is the promised Holy Spirit, and the peace that passes all understanding that comes with knowing Jesus as LORD and SAVIOR. No one who stays dead in a tomb could do all this for us. Jesus is indeed resurrected from the dead and now sits at the right hand of the Father in heaven, far above all other rulers and authorities.

Jesus, as the first fruit, was the first to rise from the dead in a resurrected body. *"In Adam all die, even so in Christ shall all be made alive, but every man in his own order, Christ the first fruits, afterward they that are Christ's at His coming."* **(1 Corinthians 15:22-24)**

In speaking of Adam, the apostle Paul is showing us that our physical bodies die; but if we are in Christ, there is a life to come even for our physical bodies. We as believers will then be the next to be bodily resurrected.

What was Jesus' resurrected body like?

"Now as the disciples said these things, Jesus Himself stood in the midst of them, and said to them, "Peace to you." But they were terrified and frightened, and supposed they had seen a spirit. And Jesus said to them, "Why are you troubled? And why do doubts arise in your hearts? Behold My hands and My feet, that it is Myself. Handle Me and see, for a spirit does not have flesh and bones as you see I have." And when He had said this, He showed them His hands and His feet. But while they still did not believe it for joy, and marveled, He said to them, "Have you any food here?" So they gave Him a piece of broiled fish and some honeycomb. And He took it and ate it in their presence." **(Luke 24:36-43)**

As we read this scripture we may think to ourselves, 'How foolish could these disciples be who had been with Jesus for over three years and then actually see Him alive, and yet act in so much unbelief?' If we had gone through all that the disciples had in the preceding 72 hours of their lives, we might act in unbelief as well.

They saw Jesus suffer on the cross. They saw the blood of Jesus drain from His body onto the ground. And finally, they saw Jesus cry out and die. For us today it may even be easier for us to believe in the resurrection, for we did not actually see the crucifixion and death of Jesus. But Jesus, in knowing and understanding all things, was patient with His disciples, showing the nail holes in His hands and the bruises on his feet. To prove that He had a real body of flesh and bone, and not just a spirit, He ate food in their presence.

"Then the same day at evening, being the first day of the week, when the doors were shut (locked) where the disciples were assembled, for fear of the Jews, Jesus came and stood in their midst, and said to them, "Peace be with you." Now when He had said this, He showed them His hands and His side. Then His disciples were glad when they saw the Lord." **(John 20:19-20)**

We see again Jesus' concern for His disciples in saying 'peace be with you' wanting to dispel the fears within them. The doors were locked, yet we see Jesus unhindered coming into the room as if the doors were open. It is apparent that the resurrected body of Jesus was extraordinary in many ways.

Jesus had flesh and bones, yet could pass through solid objects such as locked doors. He could eat food. There were still the marks of the crucifixion on His body, yet Jesus was experiencing no pain, thus indicating a now completely restored body. Is it not exciting that as believers we will receive a resurrected body of our own in which to live through all of eternity?

4.) The Physical Resurrection of Believers

Earlier in our study we found that since Christ was resurrected from the dead we are no longer separated from God. When a believer in Christ dies their soul (and spirit) go to be with Jesus in Heaven. Scripture speaks of a time yet to come in which our physical bodies will also be resurrected, just like the resurrected body of Jesus.

"But I do not want you to be ignorant, brethren, concerning those who have fallen asleep, lest you sorrow as others who have no hope. For we believe that Jesus died and rose again, even so God will bring with Him those who sleep in Jesus. For this we say to you by the Word of the Lord, that we who are alive and remain until the coming of the Lord will by no means precede those who are asleep.

For the Lord Himself will descend from heaven with a shout, with the voice of an archangel, and with the trumpet of God. And the dead in Christ will rise first. Then we who are alive and remain shall be caught up together with them in the clouds to meet the Lord in the air. And thus we shall always be with the Lord. Therefore comfort one another with these words." **(1 Thessalonians 4:13-18)**

Paul first explains to us that when a believer dies, we need not worry about them because of the hope we have in Jesus. That hope is the fact that the souls of those who believed are now with Jesus and they are very much alive (see also **2 Corinthians 5:8**). At the shout of the archangel, and the trumpet call of God, the dead in Christ (the bodies of those who have already died) will rise first. Then we who are left (believers who are still alive at his coming) will be caught up together with them in the clouds to meet the Lord in the air.

"Behold, I tell you a mystery: We shall not all sleep, but we shall all be changed - in the twinkling of an eye, at the last trumpet. For the trumpet will sound, and the dead will be raised incorruptible, and we shall be changed. For this corruptible must put on incorruption, and this mortal must put on immortality." **(1 Corinthians 15:51-53)**

NOTE: This scripture more clearly explains the changes that happen to us who are still alive at the coming of the Lord.

We will not all sleep (physically die) before the Lord returns, but we all will be changed instantly. Our mortal bodies will be changed into immortal bodies as we rise up from the earth to meet the Lord in the air. Our natural physical bodies which were growing old and deteriorating with each year of life will be instantaneously transformed into a perfect body that will live forever.

Jesus always tells the church to keep watch for no one knows the day nor the hour in which He will return. The most important thing we can do as children of God is to continue to do what God has called us to in the Great Commission until He returns for us (see **Mark 16:15**).

5.) The Physical Resurrection of Unbelievers

"Do not be amazed at this, for a time is coming when all who are in their graves will hear His voice and come out - those who have done good will rise to live, and those who have done evil will rise to be condemned." **(John 5:28-29)**

This scripture clearly shows us two different kinds of people receiving resurrected bodies. The first group refers to those who are part of the resurrection of believers that we have studied previously. The second group, who rise to be condemned, refer to the resurrection of the unbelievers which we will now study.

"Then I saw a great white throne and Him who sat on it, from whose face the earth and the heaven fled away. And there was found no place for them. And I saw the dead, small and great, standing before God, and books were opened. And another book was opened, which is the Book of Life. And the dead were judged according to their works, by things which were written in the books. The sea gave up the dead who were in it, and Death and Hades

delivered up the dead who were in them. And they were judged, each one according to his works. Then Death and Hades were cast into the lake of fire. This is the second death. And anyone not found written in the Book of Life was cast into the lake of fire. **(Revelation 20:11-15)**

Verse 12 tells us that even though these people were standing before the throne, they were still called dead (this means they were not righteous). In other words, while they were alive on the earth they had not repented of their sins and received Jesus as Lord and Savior of their lives, for this is the only way one can become righteous in God's sight. These people were judged according to what they had done while alive on the earth. If their names were not written in the Lamb's Book of Life, they were thrown into the lake of fire (this is called the second death).

The reason these people were thrown into the lake of fire was because their names were not written in the Lamb's Book of Life. But we can rejoice as spiritually resurrected (born again) believers because OUR NAMES ARE WRITTEN in the Lamb's book of life. (For further reading on this subject see **Exodus 32:33, Daniel 12:1, Malachi 3:16, Luke 10:20, Revelation 3:5,21:27,22:19**)

CONCLUSION

The doctrine of the resurrection of the dead should not be feared by Christians, but should rather be something to look forward to. When we are reunited with our resurrected body it will not be the same body as we once had. The apostle Paul tells us in **1 Corinthians 15:42** that our body is sown in the grave as perishable, but when resurrected from the grave it will be imperishable, or in other words, completely whole. No more aging, sickness or defect of any kind. Our resurrected body will be perfect in every way.

STUDY QUESTIONS (LESSON 5 - RESURRECTION OF THE DEAD)

1. Complete this scripture: *"We are confident, yes, well pleased rather to be absent from the body is…* _____".

2.What does the word resurrection mean?_____

_____

3. What must we do to be spiritually resurrected (or born again)? _____

_____

_____

4. Why is being born again the most important decision we will ever make? _____

_____

5. Before the resurrection of Christ, what two places would the souls of people go when they died? _____

_____

6. Are there any souls in Paradise <u>now</u> and explain why or why not?_____

_____

7. In your own words, can you explain why no one could go ahead of Jesus into heaven?

_____

_____

8. When Jesus returns, will we all be physically dead?_____

9. What will happen to the bodies of those believers who are still alive at the coming of the Lord?_____

_____

10. Why should an unbeliever fear death?_____

_____

_____

11. Why do we as believers not need to fear death?_____

_____

_____

NOTES

CHAPTER 6: ETERNAL JUDGMENT

"Therefore, leaving the discussion of the elementary principles of Christ, let us go on to perfection, not laying again the foundation of repentance from dead works and of faith toward God, ² of the doctrine of baptisms, of laying on of hands, of resurrection of the dead, and of eternal judgment." (Hebrews 6:1-2)

All of us will face judgment after death in the time of eternity. *"Just as a man is destined to die once, and after that to face judgment."* (Hebrews 9:27) What is eternal judgment? How are we going to be judged? Is judgment different for believers compared to unbelievers? As believers in Jesus, should we fear this judgment to come? Often when we hear the word judgment, we think of the word guilty. As believers in Jesus Christ, God does not want us to have this way of thinking as we will now see in this study.

Definition: *Judgment - Greek word, "krisis"* - To make a decision.

1.) God's Heart Concerning Judgment

"For God did not send the Son into the world in order to judge -to reject, to condemn, to pass sentence on the world; but that the world might find salvation and be made safe and sound through Him." (John 3:17 Amplified)

Jesus came on a mission from God, not to judge, but to provide a way of salvation (through His death, burial, and resurrection) so that all people might have life (see also **John 3:16**). But there is a time coming when Jesus will judge as we will see later in our study.

NOTE: The time in which we now live is called the church age or the age of grace. The word *grace* actually means unmerited favor. This unmerited favor or undeserved favor lies in the fact that our sins have been totally forgiven because of what Jesus has done for us (see **2 Corinthians 5:21**). The heart of God in this age is to bring people to Himself through His Son, Jesus.

The Woman Caught In Adultery

"Then the scribes and Pharisees brought to Him a woman caught in adultery. And when they had set her in the midst, they said to Him, "Teacher, this woman was caught in

adultery, in the very act." Now Moses, in the law, commanded us that such should be stoned. But what do You say?" This they said, testing Him, that they might have something of which to accuse Him. But Jesus stooped down and wrote on the ground with his finger, as though He did not hear.

So when they continued asking Him, He raised Himself up and said to them, "He who is without sin among you, let him throw a stone at her first." And again He stooped down and wrote on the ground. Then those who heard it, being convicted by their conscience, went out one by one, beginning with the oldest even to the last. And Jesus was left alone, and the woman standing in the midst.

When Jesus had raised Himself up and saw no one but the woman, He said to her, "Woman, where are those accusers of yours? Has no one condemned you?" She said, "No one, Lord." And Jesus came to her, "Neither do I condemn you; go and sin no more." **(John 8:3-11)**

We see that the teachers of the law and Pharisees brought this woman to Jesus in order to trap Him, because under the Mosaic Law the woman was to be stoned and they knew that Jesus would not condemn the woman. As Jesus is questioned He begins to write on the ground and then makes the statement that if there is one without sin let him throw the first stone. **Romans 3:23** tells us that, ***"all have sinned and fall short of the glory of God,"*** so none of these people were qualified to stone the woman except Jesus Christ because He was without sin. There is only one other time recorded in the bible where God wrote with His own hand.

That occasion was the writing of the Ten Commandments, which He gave to Moses (see **Exodus 24:12**). It very well could be that what Jesus was writing on the ground were the Ten Commandments, and as the teachers and Pharisees read them, they realized they were as guilty as the woman. For in the book of **James 2:10** we are told that under the Old Covenant Law, if a person broke even a small part of the Law, he was actually guilty of breaking the entire Law. The only person who had the right to stone the woman was Jesus because He was without sin. He chose not to condemn the woman and told her to go and leave her life of sin.

NOTE: Here we can see the heart of God through Jesus. He wanted to give the woman an opportunity to repent rather than condemning her to death so her soul could be saved.
"Now it came to pass, when the time had come for Him to be received up, that He steadfastly

set His face to go to Jerusalem, and sent messengers before His face. And as they went, they entered a village of the Samaritans, to prepare for Him. But they did not receive Him, because His face was set for the journey to Jerusalem. And when His disciples James and John saw this, they said, "Lord, do You want us to command fire to come down from heaven and consume them, just as Elijah did?" But He turned and rebuked them, and said, "You do not know what manner of spirit you are of. For the Son of Man did not come to destroy men's lives but to save them." And they went to another village." **(Luke 9:51-56)**

James and John wanted to call down fire from heaven to destroy a village that would not receive them. Jesus rebuked them for wanting to do this, saying that they did not know or realize the spirit in which they were speaking. This brings up a very important point of acting only upon the voice of the Spirit of God and not some other seducing spirit sent from the devil.

One of the easiest ways of discerning the difference between the voice of the Holy Spirit and a spirit from the devil is to know and understand the nature and character (heart) of God. To understand the character of God, we need to see how He acts in various situations. Since we are a New Testament church, the best place we can learn this is in the New Testament of the Bible. We serve a God who does not change. As we spend time in the Word of God and in prayer (fellowship) with Jesus, when we hear the voice of the devil we will recognize him for who he is.

"For just as the Father raises the dead and gives them life even so the Son gives life to whom He is pleased to give it. Moreover, the Father judges no one, but has entrusted all judgment to the Son." **(John 5:21-22)**

We see a time in the future when the Father raises the dead and gives them life and it is the Son (Jesus) who gives life to whom He chooses. Jesus WILL judge because the Father has given this authority to Him. What is it that pleases the Son of God that He will give us life? Only one thing, believing that Jesus Himself died on the cross for our sins and rose again from the dead, victorious over sin and death.

NOTE: We learned in our study of the resurrection of the dead that there is a time yet to come when the dead will be raised. The judgment that is spoken of in this scripture occurs after the dead are raised. In other words, this time of judgment will occur after the return of Jesus for His Church. To understand in a greater dimension that we are now in an age of grace and that a time of judgment is to come, read **Luke 4:18-20** and then read **Isaiah 61:1-6**.

Comparing these two scriptures, notice at what point Jesus stops reading, saying that what he has read is being fulfilled in their hearing. The year of the Lord's favor is now (the Church Age, the Age of Grace). But a time is coming of the Day of Vengeance (Judgment) for those who do not know Jesus.

2.) The Judgment of Believers (Judgment Seat of Christ)

"For we must all appear before the Judgment Seat of Christ, that each one may receive what is due him, for the things done while in the body, whether good or bad." **(2 Corinthians 5:10 Amplified)**

The apostle Paul is addressing believers in this scripture, so when he says 'all,' he means all believers. We will be judged according to the deeds done while in the body - the fruit of our labors. This scripture should make us ask ourselves the questions, 'What fruit was produced in my life today for the Lord Jesus Christ?' And furthermore, 'What fruit will be produced in my life tomorrow as I submit to the voice of the Holy Spirit?'

NOTE: It will not be so much what we have done, but our motives and attitudes behind our actions and our desire to know, love and serve our God.

"For no other foundation can anyone lay than that which is Jesus Christ. Now if anyone builds on this foundation with gold, silver, precious stones, wood, hay, straw, each one's work will become manifest; for the Day will declare it, because it will be revealed by fire; and the fire will test each one's work of what sort it is. If anyone's work, which he has built on it endures, he will receive a reward. If anyone's work is burned, he will suffer loss; but he himself will be saved, yet so as through fire." **(1 Corinthians 3:11-15)**

We are clearly told that our foundation is to be none other than Jesus Christ. **Hebrews 12:29** states that God is like a consuming fire. Our works done on this earth will be judged by the fire of God.

The works that are compared to hay, wood, and straw are those things done apart from the direction of God, which will be burned up by the fire of God.

The works that are compared to gold, silver, and costly stones are those things that are done under the direction and anointing of the Holy Spirit. These works will survive the fire of God and will be rewarded on that DAY (at the Judgment Seat of Christ). If a believer's works are burned up he will still be saved, but will suffer loss with no rewards. We should be thankful as believers that God does purge us; for if He did not do this, we would not be able to enter His presence, for nothing impure or unholy can enter His presence.

"But why do you judge your brother? Or why do you show contempt for your brother? For we shall all stand before the judgment seat of Christ. For it is written: "As I live, says the LORD, every knee shall bow to Me, and every tongue shall confess to God." So then each of us shall give account of himself to God. Therefore let us not judge one another anymore but rather resolve this, not to put a stumbling block or a cause to fall in our brother's way." **(Romans 14:10-13)**

We are not to judge our brother to condemn him, but rather, if we see a brother in sin we should take actions to help him be restored. As Christians we will have to stand before the Judgment Seat of God (Christ) to give an account for our actions. Do you think that Jesus is pleased with all of our actions today, or do we need to make some changes? Our heart should not put any kind of hindrance (roadblock) in our brother's way that could cause him to fall, but rather find ways to make his path straight to the honor and glory of God.

"For the time has come for judgment to begin at the house of God; and if it begins with us first, what will be the end of those who do not obey the Gospel of God? Now if the righteous one is scarcely saved, where will the ungodly and the sinner appear?" **(1 Peter 4:17-18)**

We see that the house of God (believers) will be judged first and after this will be the judgment of the ungodly and sinner. Keep in mind that the word judgment means to make a right decision.

The Parable of the Talents

"For the kingdom of heaven is like a man traveling to a far country, who called his own servants and delivered his goods to them. And to one he gave five talents, to another two, and to another one, to each according to his own ability; and immediately he went on a journey. Then he who had received the five talents went and traded with them, and made another five talents. And likewise he who had received two gained two more also. But he who had received one went and dug in the ground, and hid his lord's money. After a long time the lord of those servants came and settled accounts with them. So he who had received five talents came and brought five other talents, saying, "Lord, you delivered to me five talents; look, I have gained five more talents besides them."

His lord said to him, "Well done, good and faithful servant; you were faithful over a few things, I will make you ruler over many things. Enter into the joy of your lord." He also who had received two talents came and said, "Lord, you delivered to me two talents; look, I have gained two more talents besides them." His lord said to him, "Well done, good and faithful servant; you have been faithful over a few things, I will make you ruler over many things. Enter into the joy of your lord."

Then he who had received the one talent came and said, "Lord, I knew you to be a hard man, reaping where you have not sown, and gathering where you have not scattered seed. And I was afraid, and went and hid your talent in the ground. Look, there you have what is yours." But his lord answered and said to him, "You wicked and lazy servant, you knew that I reap where I have not sown, and gather where I have not scattered seed. Therefore you ought to have deposited my money with the bankers, and at my coming I would have received back my own with interest.

Therefore take the talent from him, and give it to him who has ten talents. For to everyone who has more will be given, and he will have abundance; but from him who does not have, even what he has will be taken away. And cast the unprofitable servant into the outer darkness. There will be weeping and gnashing of teeth." **(Matthew 25:14-30)**

As we read this parable we see that there are those who are faithful with what God has given them, and those who abuse what God gives to them. Our heart's desire should be like the good and faithful servant so that when we are called to give an accounting of the works done while in the body (at the Judgment Seat of Christ), that our Master (Jesus Christ) will say to each one of us, "Well done good and faithful servant! You have been faithful with a few things; I will put you in charge of many things. Come and share your Master's happiness."

There will be no greater reward than to hear Jesus speak those words to us as individuals who took what God had given us in this life and invested it in the advancement of the Kingdom. For in so doing, we are storing up treasures for ourselves in heaven that neither moth nor rust may destroy, and thieves cannot break in and steal. Let none of us be like the wicked and lazy servant who took what his master had given him and did nothing with it, losing even that when his master returned.

3.) Judgment of Unbelievers (Great White Throne Judgment)

The Parable of the Sheep and the Goats

"When the Son of Man comes in His glory, and all the holy angels with Him, then He will sit on the throne of His glory. All the nations will be gathered before Him, and He will separate them one from another, as a shepherd divides his sheep from the goats. And He will set the sheep on His right hand, but the goats on the left. Then the King will say to those on His right hand, "Come, you blessed of My Father, inherit the kingdom prepared for you from the foundation of the world: For I was hungry and you gave me food; I was thirsty and you gave Me drink; I was a stranger and you took Me in; I was naked and you clothed Me; I was sick and you visited Me; I was in prison and you came to Me."

Then the righteous will answer Him, saying, "Lord, when did we see You hungry and feed You, or thirsty and give You drink? When did we see You a stranger and take You in, or naked and clothe You?" Or when did we see You sick, or in prison, and come to you?" And the King will answer and say to them, "Assuredly, I say to you, inasmuch as you did it to one of the least of these My brethren, you did it to Me." Then He will also say to those on the left hand, "Depart from Me, you cursed, into the everlasting fire prepared for the devil and his angels.

For I was hungry and you gave Me no food; I was thirsty and you gave Me no drink; I was a stranger and you did not take Me in, naked and you did not clothe Me, sick and in prison and you did not visit Me." Then they also will answer Him, saying, "Lord, when did we see You hungry, or thirsty, or a stranger, or naked, or sick, or in prison, and did not minister to You?" Then He will answer them, saying, "Assuredly, I say to you, inasmuch as you did not do it to one of the least of these, you did not do it to Me." And these will go away into everlasting punishment, but the righteous into eternal life." **(Matthew 25:31-46)**

We see that the believers are the sheep and the unbelievers are goats. The believers (sheep) are judged first (see also **1 Peter 4:17-18**). Earlier in our study we saw that the heart of God was for none to perish (go to hell), but that all should come to repentance. I often hear unbelievers say to me they cannot believe in a God who would send anyone to hell. We see in verse 41 these unbelievers are cursed and thrown into the lake of fire that had been prepared for the devil and his angels. What had hell been created and prepared for? The devil, and his evil angels, and not for humans at all. Then why does God send people there? The truth of the matter is that God has *never* sent anyone to hell. People send themselves there when they refuse the free gift of Jesus Christ, who was sent to save all people because God loved the entire world and provided the gift of salvation for all mankind through Him. Because they refused the free gift of salvation and did not heed the voice of God, they will receive their due penalty for their iniquity (sin of rebellion), which is the lake of fire (see also **John 8:31, 10:27-29 Amplified**).

"Then I saw a Great White Throne and Him who was seated on it, earth and sky fled from His presence, and there was no place for them. And I saw the DEAD, great and small, standing before the throne, and books were opened. Another book was opened, which is the Book of Life. The DEAD were judged according to what they had done as recorded in the books.

The sea gave up the dead that were in it, and death and hades gave up the dead that were in them, and each person was judged according to what they had done. Then death and hades were thrown into the lake of fire. The lake of fire is the second death. If anyone's name was not found in the Book of Life, he was thrown into the lake of fire." **(Revelation 20:11-15)**

We know from **John 5:22** that the one seated on the throne will be Jesus, as all judgment has been given to Him. Each will be judged according to what they had done as recorded in books; and if their names are not found in the Book of Life they will be cast into the lake of fire, which is called the second death. There are several books mentioned in this scripture.

The first books have all the works done in this life recorded in them. Everything that was ever done by the unbeliever or even thought is recorded in these books, which will be opened and read at the Great White Throne Judgment.

The unbeliever's own words and actions of unbelief toward Jesus will condemn them on the last day, sending them to the lake of fire. The second book mentioned called the Book of Life has recorded the names of those who are believers. Is it not wonderful that when we confess our sins and receive forgiveness through the blood of Jesus, all that was recorded in the first set of books is erased. For the word *forgive* actually means forgetting what the sin was.

Man may never have the capability to forgive and forget, but God does, even to the extent that if you brought up past sins that you have repented of, God would ask you what you were talking about. He has forgiven and forgotten them!

What sin(s) will be the ones that condemn these people to the lake of fire?

"And this is the testimony: that God has given us eternal life, and this life is in His Son. He who has the Son has life; he who does not have the Son of God does not have life." **(1 John 5:11-12)**

The testimony of God is this: Eternal life is found in the Son of God - if the Son is in you, you have eternal life. Apart from the Son of God you will not have eternal life with God, for without Jesus and His perfect blood sacrifice for your sins you have no right to enter the presence of an almighty holy God.

"Whoever believes in the Son has eternal life, but whoever rejects the Son will not see life, for God's wrath remains on him." **(John 3:36)**

NOTE: Even though the unbeliever will have to give a complete accounting of his life at the Great White Throne Judgment, it will only be one sin that will send him into the lake of fire. This sin is the sin of unbelief concerning the finished work of Christ (see **Matthew 12:31-37, Romans 10:9:10**).

CONCLUSION

As born again believers in Jesus we need not fear the time of eternal judgment to come. Our salvation does not depend on the works done in the body, but is a free gift through faith in Jesus Christ (see **Ephesians 2:8-10**). Does this mean that we can live slack and unproductive lives? Of course not. As followers of Jesus we want to please our heavenly Father who loves us and desires us to be overcomers in this life. God wants us to be living testimonies of the redeeming work of His Son, Jesus (see **Galatians 3:13**).

For unbelievers, the story is different. They will be judged guilty because of unbelief in Jesus and the end result of this is eternal torment in the lake of fire.

Has this study given you a greater desire to share your faith in Jesus? **John 14:6** tells us, *"Jesus is the way and the truth and the life. No one comes to the Father except by Him."* As believers in Jesus, we have the key to eternal life. Jesus has left us here on the earth that we might share this key with the lost people around us, so that they might be born again through the free gift of Jesus, and gain entrance into the kingdom of God.

STUDY QUESTIONS   (LESSON 6 - ETERNAL JUDGMENT)

1. Are all people going to face judgment?_____

2. What does the word "judge" mean?_____

3. What must occur first before the time of Eternal Judgment?(See Heb. 9:27)_____
_____

4. In your own words, can you state the reasons why Jesus was sent into the world?
_____
_____

5. Can you give an example from scripture that shows us the heart of God in this age of grace, the church age?_____
_____

6. Name the two eternal Judgments that will occur, stating who will be judged and the outcome of each group._____
_____
_____
_____

7. At the Judgment Seat of Christ, why will our works done in the body be judged?
_____

8. Is our salvation an issue at the Judgment Seat of Christ? Why or why not?
_____
_____

9. At the Great White Throne Judgment, what one sin will condemn these people to hell and why?_____
_____

10. In your own words, what do you feel that Jesus wants us to do as we await his return and why?
_____
_____
_____

NOTES

BIBLIOGRAPHY

1. VINE'S EXPOSITORY DICTIONARY

   W. E. Vine   Oliphants Ltd. 1940   One Volume 1952

2. STRONG'S EXHAUSTIVE CONCORDANCE

   James Strong, S.T.D.,LL.D.   Copyright 1890, by James Strong   Madison, N.J.

3. THE SPIRIT FILLED BELIEVERS

   Derek Prince   HANDBOOK   Creation House Strang Com.   Company Florida, 1993

4. THE COMPLETE WORD STUDY

   Spios Zodhiates Th.D.   NEW TESTAMENT   AMG Publishers 1991

5. THE COMPARATIVE STUDY BIBLE (King James Version) (The Amplified Bible)
   (New American Standard) (New International Version) The Zondervan Corp. 1984
   Grand Rapids Mich. 49506

Made in the USA
Middletown, DE
26 September 2020